GARDENING
THE AMANA WAY

A Bur Oak Book

HOLLY CARVER, SERIES EDITOR

GARDENING

the Amana Way

LAWRENCE L. RETTIG

UNIVERSITY OF IOWA PRESS • IOWA CITY

University of Iowa Press, Iowa City 52242

Copyright © 2013 by the University of Iowa Press

www.uiowapress.org

Printed in the United States of America

Design by April Leidig

The University of Iowa Press is a member of Green Press Initiative
and is committed to preserving natural resources.

Printed on acid-free paper

Library of Congress Cataloging-in-Publication Data

Rettig, Lawrence L.

Gardening the Amana way / by Lawrence L. Rettig. — 1st ed.

p.   cm. — (A bur oak book)

Includes bibliographical references and index.

ISBN: 978-1-60938-190-5, 1-60938-190-4 (pbk.)

ISBN 978-1-60938-219-3, 1-60938-219-6 (ebook)

1. Amana Society. 2. Gardens — Iowa — Amana. 3. Gardening —
Iowa — Amana. 4. Gardening — Iowa — Amana — History.

I. Title. II. Series: Bur oak book.

SB453.2.I8R48 2013

635.09777′653 — dc23   2013010112

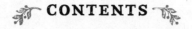

CONTENTS

Acknowledgments • vii

Preface • ix

1
The Community of True Inspiration • 1

2
The Evolution of Communal Gardening in Amana • 11

3
Gardening in Old Amana • 17

4
Vegetable Gardening in Modern Amana • 43

5
Flower Gardening in Modern Amana • 53

6
Favorite Plants in Cottage-in-the-Meadow Gardens • 65

7
Creativity in and out of the Gardens • 81

8
Gardening Indoors • 107

Botanical Names of Plants in This Book • 111

References • 115

Index • 117

❦ ACKNOWLEDGMENTS ❦

THIS BOOK IS DEDICATED to my lovely wife, Wilma, fellow gardener and life partner for these past fifty years, and to the generations of communal women gardeners who preceded her.

I am indebted to fellow authors and Amana Society members Emilie Hoppe and Peter Hoehnle for their valuable and painstaking research: Emilie for documentation of everyday life in communal Amana, especially as it relates to gardening, and Peter for his documentation of the history associated with the Amana Lily Lake and the Amana sojourn of Joseph Prestele Sr.

Content previously published on the Dave's Garden website is used here with permission.

❧ PREFACE ❧

ARDENING IN THE seven villages of Iowa's Amana Colonies is a culmi-
nation of gardening techniques, and gardening in general, that stretch
back several centuries to Central Europe. It was a natural outcome of the
need to provide food for a growing number of adherents to a new faith called
Die Gemeinde der Wahren Inspiration (The Community of True Inspiration).
Persecution for its beliefs forced this new subculture to form its own communities and provide its own food sources for mutual survival and protection.
This book traces Inspirationist communal gardening and the communal
spirit from its beginnings in Europe to its continuing evolution in the Inspirationists' new homes here in the United States. We'll see how they worked
together in their gardens, orchards, and fields to produce enough food to
feed themselves and what became of their gardens when inner turmoil and
the Great Depression caused the breakdown of communal life. As a child
of parents who were part of communal life in the Amana Society and as an
heir to the Amana gardening tradition, I'll show you how my gardening has
been influenced by that tradition and how it differs from it. We'll explore the
founding of Cottage-in-the Meadow Gardens as well as the philosophy that
drives it. I've included lots of information on the plants that my wife and I
grow in these gardens.

Finally, I'll offer some how-tos for gardeners interested in my methods as
well as recipes that take advantage of the produce we raise. Crafters using
plant material in their creations will find some interesting projects here, too.

Plants, methods, projects, whatever your gardening passions are, I hope
you'll find this book interesting and informative. Please feel free to contact
me if you have questions or comments. You can reach me at Cottage-in-
the-Meadow Gardens, P.O. Box 107, South Amana, IA 52334, or at rettigs@
southslope.net.

GARDENING
THE AMANA WAY

THE COMMUNITY OF
TRUE INSPIRATION

GOOGLE THE WORD "Amana," and you'll quickly discover that it's associated with an amazing assortment of items. Falling under its rubric is an Islamic mutual fund, a collection of appliances, the name of a Hebrew mountain, a street in Honolulu, an academy in Georgia, a society, a corporation, a place in Iowa. It's the latter three in this litany that relate to our exploration of gardening in Amana.

Amana's gardening legacy is built upon a rich history that reaches back in time to the early eighteenth century. The year 1714 found Eberhard Ludwig Gruber and Johann Friedrich Rock deeply dissatisfied with the orthodox Lutheran faith in the German province of Hesse and with the clergy who expounded it. Gruber and Rock wanted a more personalized religion, one that resembled the tenets of Pietism, a popular movement sweeping Europe at the time. They believed in the divine inspiration of the Bible and, more importantly, that God could and would communicate His will through inspired prophets still today. Gruber and Rock became those prophets.

Calling themselves Inspirationists, the duo preached their doctrine of divine inspiration throughout Germany and as far south as Switzerland, founding small cells of the new sect as they went. During the remainder of the century, the movement ebbed and flowed.

The early years of a new century saw a strong and growing revival of Inspirationism. So vigorous was this renewed enthusiasm that authorities and the general citizenry often viewed the movement as a threat to established socio-religious norms. They shunned the established church and believed that God could communicate directly with them through the divine inspiration of some of the sect's leaders, called *Werkzeuge* (in this instance, meaning "tools of the Lord"). On occasion, Inspirationists were flogged, stoned, spat upon, or even jailed when they dared to venture out into the streets.

This persecution grew so severe that members of the sect began to abandon their homes and band together for mutual support and protection. A sympathetic prince in the province of Hesse opened his castle, the Ronneburg, to the beleaguered folk. Here they lived, gardened, and ate as a community, pooling their resources. When there was no longer room to accommodate the continuing influx of members, the community purchased other estates in the surrounding countryside to house them.

Persecution continued to be an issue, compounded in 1842 by a catastrophic crop failure. It was during this time that a new and charismatic leader, Christian Metz, arose. In one of his divine testimonies, he declared that salvation for the movement lay across the sea to the west. This was interpreted to mean the United States, most likely because large-scale emigration to the United States was in progress in Western Europe during the 1830s and 1840s. More important, though, was the fact that the United States represented the embodiment of religious tolerance.

In 1842, several leaders from the Inspirationist community set sail for the state of New York. In short order, they purchased a tract of land just west of Buffalo totaling about 5,000 acres, later acquiring 3,000 more. Progress was swift. By 1843, the elders had laid out three small villages that the increasing flow of immigrant Inspirationists soon filled to capacity.

The governing elders ultimately organized six villages as the communal Ebenezer Society, making official the lifestyle that was born of necessity in their German homeland. Elders in the new communities ruled the enterprise and assigned members to the tasks at hand. In choosing to live communally, members of the Ebenezer Society joined a growing list of communal and utopian societies taking root in the United States during the eighteenth and nineteenth centuries. The 1800s alone produced almost 200 such endeavors. Many were ephemeral, fading from the scene in just a few years.

Ebenezer, surviving dissonance and disease, actually grew and prospered for nearly fifteen years. Elders ordered additional villages built to accommodate the continuing influx of Inspirationists from Europe. By 1854 the population topped 1,200.

As one of the main ports of entry for immigrants, the city of Buffalo was booming. This eventually posed a dilemma for the Ebenezer Society. The increase in the Society's population over the years required continued expansion, but the available land in the area had become much more expensive due to Buffalo's westward growth. Elders who ran Ebenezer also worried that the close proximity of a large city's "worldly" society would have a negative impact on the Society's morality and spirituality. Once again, the elders came to believe that salvation lay to the west.

In November of 1854, the community elders appointed an inspection committee and charged it with finding a new home for the Ebenezer Society. On one of these searches, the committee journeyed westward to Iowa City, located in the east central part of the new state of Iowa. They chose an ideal site approximately 25 miles to the west with the help of local land agents who accompanied them in their search and gave them advice. The soil in this area was extremely fertile, the bluffs above the river valley were heavily wooded, and there were sandstone outcroppings for quarrying and clay deposits suitable for brick making.

The elders soon made the official decision to move Ebenezer to Iowa. The move was a gradual one, accomplished over a period of eight years, from 1855 to 1862. In that same period, the Inspirationists' new home grew to encompass seven villages located on 26,000 acres, much of which consisted of ultra fertile farmland and lush forests. Amana was the first village built, named after a mountain mentioned in one of the biblical songs of Solomon. Five of the six other village names have the name Amana as an appendage: East Amana, High Amana, Middle Amana, South Amana, and West Amana. Homestead, the seventh village, was already named when the Inspirationists bought it. It was an outpost with a rail connection considered advantageous to the economy of the new communal enterprise.

Settling the Amanas, as the villages are called collectively, was generally an orderly process in which the elders reigned supreme over both secular and religious affairs. Residents lived in assigned quarters, ate in communal kitchens, and worked daily—with the exception of Sundays—at their assigned tasks. Each village had its own church, farm fields, farm animals, orchards, vineyards, kitchen gardens, kitchen houses, school, bakery, dairy, wine cellar, post office, sawmill, and general store. The elders located woolen mills and flour mills in the villages of Amana, Middle Amana, and West Amana.

As in Ebenezer, the elders set up an official government, producing a constitution and a new name, the Amana Society. During the next seven decades

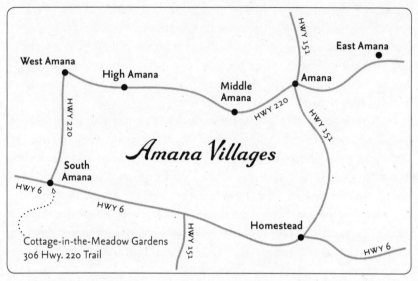

Amana Villages showing Cottage-in-the-Meadow Gardens location.

from 1855 to 1932, the members of the Society lived a simple, religious, communal life of isolation. Farms, factories, stores, crafts, and communal gardens prospered.

A typical day in the life of Amana Society residents, during this time, began with breakfast at the communal kitchen to which elders assigned them, with about forty members to each kitchen. Then it was off to the assigned tasks for the day. That might be preparing the rest of the daily meals; hauling manure to the fields; planting and tending crops; making baskets, tin ware, or pottery; smoking meats; tailoring clothes; doing leather work; making cherry and walnut furniture; or working in the woolen and flour mills or in the calico factory. There was generally a work and food break at mid-morning and again after the noon meal at mid-afternoon. During the growing season, workers in the fields and in the kitchen gardens got special attention from the kitchen sisters, who prepared their snacks delivered by horse and wagon to wherever the laborers happened to be located in the fields.

After the evening meal, the day wasn't yet over. Elders conducted prayer meetings every evening at various locations around each village. There were also religious services in the main church building on Wednesday and

Field hands enjoy a mid-morning snack,
courtesy of one of the communal kitchens.

Sunday mornings and sometimes in the afternoons as well. Not counting religious holiday observances, there were generally eleven services in each village every week.

It's important to note that life in the Amanas was definitely not all work and church attendance with no play. In the spring, summer, and fall, members went on picnics, went fishing, gathered bouquets of wild flowers, and took long walks in the countryside during their spare time. The more adventurous among the younger men went swimming in the various ponds, in the seven-mile-long millrace built by the colonists to power woolen mills and smaller enterprises, and in the Iowa River that meandered through the valley. In the winter there was ice-skating, sled riding, and gliding about in a horse-drawn sleigh. The whole year through, the kitchen workers sang as they worked. The men sang in choruses called *Sängerbunde* and did wood-crafting, and everyone read books—primarily the Bible, the testimonies of the *Werkzeuge*, and other religious works printed by the Print Shop in Middle Amana. Nonreligious reading was available, but only in school books and in a few other more secular materials passed on from family to family.

Young women fish in the millrace. The distinctive bridges over this seven-mile-long canal were designed to open up so that a steam operated dredge could pass through.

Amana men taking a refreshing dip.

Pre-1932 baseball team in South Amana.

The list of leisure time activities wouldn't be complete without a word about baseball, originally a forbidden leisure time activity. As part of the youth rebellion of the 1920s, young men played the game surreptitiously on makeshift diamonds in the woods. Eventually, community elders dropped their opposition, and the first real ball field appeared in Middle Amana in the late 1920s.

The heavily structured society changed little during this period. But a changing world outside the confines of this isolated society eventually broke down its barriers. New technologies like the automobile, the telephone, and the radio represented serious challenges to the secluded Amana Society.

By the 1920s, visitors in automobiles were flocking to the Amanas—breaching the Society's social barriers—to spend the day among these quaint folks who dressed in dark clothing and called each other *Bruder* and *Schwester* (brother and sister). Following an old Germanic dictate that visitors must be welcomed, fed, and housed if necessary, word soon spread through the region about these gracious folks, their wonderful food served in their communal kitchen houses, the quaint architecture, and the bucolic setting.

The proverbial Pandora's Box had been opened. Although the village elders—charged with seeing to both the spiritual and the physical needs of

Visitors in the early 1900s tour Amana.

their fellow members—tried to stem the flow, it was not to be. The younger members, especially, liked what they saw. Compared to the colorful clothing that visitors wore, their dark pants, dresses, and suits—standard issue in the Society—seemed drab and lifeless. Female visitors with bobbed hair drew the interest of the Society's younger women.

It wasn't long before members realized that a little forbidden capitalism would earn them pocket money. They sold visitors fruit from their trees and gardens or perhaps a piece of beautiful walnut furniture that they could do without. A parlor organ or a crystal radio set might then mysteriously appear in the family living room. Hard feelings began to grow between the haves and the have-nots.

By the mid-1920s, it was obvious to almost everyone that the communal lifestyle was seriously threatened. Young folks yearned for the standard of living they observed outside their community's borders. Eventually, it came to open rebellion. Even though it was considered a sin to do so, young women began to bob their hair. Young men often refused to work, saying they were ill and couldn't carry out their assigned duties.

Village elders worked long and hard to find a solution. They realized that maintaining the society that they established so long ago in Ebenezer was no longer an option. Too many factors worked against that option: loss of charismatic leadership, gradual abandonment of the philosophy of isolation from the outside world, and financial problems aggravated by social unrest locally and a deepening economic depression nationally. On June 1, 1932, the old order came to an end. Put to a vote by the Society's adult population, a new plan was approved by over 90 percent of the voters.

Gone were the *Gardebaas*, the *Kichebaas*, the *Farm Mennetscher*, and their staffs mentioned in chapter 3. A far more secular society came into being, almost the antithesis of the communal life members had led. The old society morphed into one that was a joint stock corporation organized for profit. The new corporation issued shares to members over the age of twenty-one, according to the number of years they had served the communal enterprise. Another share, the Class A share, was restricted to a single share per person. It served as the voting share and assured that no one person or group could buy up shares and gain control of the corporation. Tacked onto this share was a holdover from the communal life that provided the bearer with free medical, dental, and burial services.

Known as the Great Change, this venture transformed the Amana lifestyle forever. For the first time in Inspirationist history, the new Articles of Incorporation separated church and state. The newly formed Amana Society, Inc., served as the corporate entity, and the new Amana Church Society continued to serve the spiritual needs of the community. Services were still conducted in German, and women continued to wear their traditional black church garb: a cap that tied under the chin, an apron, and a shawl.

This radical transformation was just what the people needed. Men who refused to work due to illness experienced miraculous recoveries. They sought out jobs in the new corporation or commuted to nearby Cedar Rapids and Iowa City. Cashing in nonvoting shares plus a steady hourly wage allowed them and the rest of their compatriots to purchase automobiles and the houses and lots where they were already living during the Great Change. They had to set up kitchens in their homes since the communal kitchens closed when the new order took effect.

Private enterprises that weren't part of the new corporation began to appear in the various villages. Perhaps the most notable was Amana Refrigeration, Inc., a producer of appliances founded by Amana native George Foerstner. Both Amana Refrigeration, Inc., and the Amana Society, Inc., had their ups and downs. Although neither one much resembles its earlier corporate image, both are still in business today.

The modern Amana Society corporation split its Class A stock one hundred to one in 1972, the new shares no longer bearing the privilege of free medical, dental and burial services. Old Class A shares were still honored, but new issues no longer carried those benefits. From time to time, it has divested itself of a business operating under its umbrella but has also added new ones. Foerstner's Amana appliance factory has been sold numerous times since its founding. At the time of this writing, it's owned by the Whirlpool Corporation, considered the world's leading manufacturer and marketer of major home appliances.

And what of the people who call the Amana villages home today? They lead lives very similar to people in other small towns and villages across the country. The population numbers have remained remarkably steady over the years, fluctuating between 1,500 and 1,800, currently at approximately 1,700. What has changed is the composition of that population. "Outsiders," as Amana natives tend to call them (though generally without any derogatory connotation), make up a good portion of today's Amana villages. Marriages to outsiders, the pursuit of higher education, and the search for good, meaningful jobs have depleted the native population. Actually, outsiders generally embrace Amana's culture, both present and past. They're often active in preserving and promoting both cultures.

It's important to note that the arts (especially painting in various media) have blossomed in the post-communal era as have music and numerous crafts. I find it amazing that so many artistic talents had lain dormant in communal Amana and now have found their expression in the post-1932 culture. Outsiders have contributed to this trend, adding their artistic interpretations of Amana as well as pursuing their favorite crafts and learning new ones.

As I write this, the economy here is subdued, as it is across the whole country. Amana Society, the corporation, paid no dividends this year as a result. But tourists still visit in droves, and the countryside in this lush river valley is as beautiful as ever. All pastures and forestland owned by the Amana Society comprise a game preserve that supports a wealth of plant and animal life. Those erstwhile communal garden plots today support lots of grassy lawns and pastures, flowers common to everyday gardening in the Midwest, and a smattering of vegetable gardens.

THE EVOLUTION OF
COMMUNAL GARDENING
IN AMANA

T O UNDERSTAND THE origins of Amana gardening, we need to travel back in time to the early 1800s, when the Inspirationists were, of necessity, living a de facto communal life in Germany in the province of Hesse. While there's no detailed evidence of how the Inspirationists gardened back then, we do find mention now and then of various food-associated garden plants and of crop failure.

The historical record gets a bit more detailed with the move from Germany to Ebenezer, New York, beginning in 1842. We know that members of the Ebenezer Society ate in communal kitchens and that the produce for those meals came primarily from the crops they planted in fields and in gardens within the villages. It's not until the move to Amana that we find many aspects of gardening recorded in great detail.

And, interestingly, we discover that the elders grudgingly permitted the growing of decorative plants, thanks to the influence of Joseph Prestele Sr.

There's no question that Prestele deserves a place of honor in a book about Amana gardening. He, more than any other person, is responsible for the introduction of flower gardening into a culture that frowned upon such unproductive, non-utilitarian plantings. To understand how this came about, we need to know a bit about Prestele's life.

Joseph Prestele Sr. was born in the German town of Jettingen, Bavaria, in 1796. After he completed his schooling in the village, he most likely gained his detailed knowledge of garden plants, their propagation, and their care from the proprietor of a local nursery. It's also likely that Prestele became acquainted with the orchard, the vegetable gardens, and the flower beds of

Count von Staufenberg's nearby estate, where his father was employed as a caretaker.

As a young adult, Prestele came to live in Munich. Having shown considerable artistic ability, he soon developed an interest in lithography, a method for printing images etched into limestone that had originated in Munich in the year of his birth. It was an interest that became a dominant factor throughout the rest of his life.

After a stint in the army, Prestele was discharged in September of 1823. In October of that year he married Karolina Russ. She bore nine children, five of whom survived to adulthood. Prestele was hired by King Ludwig of Bavaria to tend to the king's gardens, later becoming head gardener for the estate. That position provided him with a virtually unlimited source of subjects for his plant lithographs, which he colored using watercolor as the medium. It's obvious that he was well liked at court, as Ludwig encouraged him to get a university education and supported him financially as he studied art at the University of Vienna. As a result, Prestele soon earned a reputation as a respected and gifted lithographer.

Although he was born a Catholic, Prestele's continual search for a more personal and meaningful form of worship eventually led him and his family to Engelthal, one of a number of estates occupied by the Community of True Inspiration in the province of Hesse. For Prestele, this was truly an answer to his prayers. Not only did Inspirationism speak to his spiritual needs, it provided food and shelter for him and his family. Prestele had fallen on hard times, having been dismissed as head gardener at court as the result of a regime change. He was unable to earn enough money from his lithographs to provide what he considered an acceptable standard of living for his family.

Prestele's health was also a major factor in his life. During a brief incarceration for his religious beliefs, Prestele became quite ill. As a result, he was allowed a half hour each day to exercise in the fresh air of the police garrison's courtyard. Historians agree that he most likely suffered from tuberculosis. He was haunted by it throughout his life, sometimes faring better, other times worse.

Within five years after joining the Inspirationist group, Prestele found himself preparing for a mass emigration to the United States. He and his family arrived in the fall of 1843, while the main village of Ebenezer was still

under construction. The crossing, which took more than fifty days, had been
a nightmare for him. He was violently ill almost the entire time, so much so
that the captain took pity on him and allowed him to sleep in his quarters
and take his meals there whenever he was able to eat something.

Upon his arrival in Ebenezer, Prestele found, to his great joy, that workers
had already completed his house, so he and his family could move in immediately. Once settled, he began producing lithographs again, selling them
to the likes of Asa Gray (considered the most important American botanist
of the 19th century), the U.S. government, the Smithsonian Institution, and
various prominent nurserymen. At that time, he was considered the most
well-known and gifted lithographer in the whole country. All proceeds from
the sale of his work went directly into the communal treasury.

For his own pleasure, Prestele created a garden in the space around his
new home. That in itself wasn't unusual, since other houses in Ebenezer had
gardens as well. What made his garden unique was the fact that aside from
several peach and pear trees, he had planted flowers. All gardens in the village were to be utilitarian, producing food for the commune. Flowers were a
frivolity not tolerated by the Society's elders.

Not only did Prestele plant flowers, he also created a *Rawatt* (standard
German *Rabatte*, a raised bed with a heavy plank frame holding in the soil)
about four or five feet wide along the foundation of all four sides of his house.
Here he planted mainly vining varieties such as morning glories, climbing
beans, and sweet peas. He also built several wooden trellises and attached
them directly to the outside walls of the house to support the vines.

Why was Prestele allowed to break the rules? There are a number of plau-
sible reasons. He used the flowers as subjects for his lithographs. His lithographs were an important source of income for the commune. He was a village
elder. He was a good friend of Christian Metz, the charismatic Inspirationist
leader. His former position at the court of a king elevated his social standing.

Although Prestele was allowed a privilege others couldn't enjoy, he was
required to provide some sweat equity. In early 1844 he was put in charge
of caring for an apple orchard established by the former Native American
occupants whom the U.S. government had just driven from the land. In addition, he was assigned the task of creating a nursery, where fruit trees could
be propagated. The catch was that he actually had to clear a plot for the nurs-

Wooden plank *Rawatt* with native fern planting.

Prestele-style trellises still grace the south and west walls of many Amana homes today. Note the grapes on the trellis and the old-fashioned petunias growing in the *Rawatt* beneath it.

ery in the virgin forest that surrounded the community. Given his delicate
health, this was a monumental undertaking.

By the time summer arrived, it became obvious that his health wouldn't
allow Prestele to continue such heavy labor. He also missed his artwork. In
Prestele's mind, what followed was truly divine intervention. Two elders paid
him a visit, bringing news that a decision had been made to assign him once
more to creating lithographs. Although there's no direct evidence to vali-
date this, one could easily conclude that, since the communal treasury could
benefit from the income Prestele provided through the sale of his works of
art, producing lithographs took priority over creating a nursery at that point.

Of critical importance to the evolution of flower gardening in the Ebenezer villages and later in the Amanas is the fact that Prestele shared some of
his flowering plants with fellow members and that a *Rawatt* or a trellis or two
soon appeared at the homes of others.

Prestele and his family arrived in the village of Amana from Ebenezer in
the fall of 1858. Once settled, Prestele began to realize how remote his location was from his former customers along the East Coast. Far worse, color
printing was a fast-developing new technique, rendering his beautiful litho-
graphed, watercolor plant images almost obsolete. His career as an illustrator
of major works was essentially over.

To get an indication of how strong Prestele's flower gardening influence
was on the community by the time the Amana villages were built, one need
only look at the trellises that decorated practically every building in the new
settlement. Almost all residential houses soon had *Rawatte* as well, with flowers filling many of them. *Rawatte* were originally constructed of wood. Once
concrete became available, it was the material of choice. Exceptions include
several constructed with limestone.

One of Prestele's joys in his new environment, and one of the first things
he did upon arrival in Amana, was to establish a new garden. Its location
was on the western edge of the village in an area of rich soil and close to
Price Creek, which offered a convenient water supply. Amana historian Peter
Hoehnle describes the garden:

> Prestele had a knowledge of plants that was unusual for its depth and
> breadth at the time. He not only knew common species, but through his
> scientific work, all manner of the new varieties of apples, plums, pears,

and roses being developed, as well as the unusual plants brought back by government expeditions to the far west. This was not your average orchard, vegetable, or flower garden but a living museum, an arboretum, of growing things of all different types.

The illness that had dogged Prestele most of his life finally overwhelmed him in 1867 at the age of seventy-one. He lies buried in the Amana Cemetery on a slight incline which, to the north, overlooks the site of his cherished garden. And what of that garden? Peter Hoehnle explains:

Slowly, year by year, Prestele's untended garden melted back into the soil. The last tree, a gnarled spruce, died in 1950, almost a century after it was planted. Its death did not go unnoticed: a photograph and a short article about it were printed, and then it was gone. Prestele's garden became a corn field, just as it had once been open prairie.

3

GARDENING
IN OLD AMANA

I F YOU HAVE EVER HAD the good fortune of raising your own vegetables, you know how wonderful they taste when they're whisked out of the
garden and onto the table in short order. Imagine the coordinated effort
it would take to accomplish that act for an entire village, to say nothing of
seven villages. The Amana settlers did just that, and they did it well.

Fuelling the bustling activity in the seven villages was the wonderful
food prepared in the communal kitchens. The kitchens, in turn, depended
on the communal gardens for many of the dishes they served. This meant
that the lives and duties of the *Kichebaas* (kitchen boss) and the *Gardebaas*
(garden boss) were tightly interwoven. They cooperated with one another
in a friendly, helpful manner, but each one ruled over her own domain with
great authority, a somewhat stern demeanor, and a kind heart. The *Gardebaas* also conferred with the *Farm Mennetscher*, who was in charge of the
village farming operation, which included preparing the garden plots for
planting in spring and planting and harvesting the potato and onion fields.

Elders assigned each kitchen a plot of land—usually two or three acres—
on which to raise its produce. Villages had anywhere from three to twelve
communal kitchens, depending on the size of the village. In all, about 100
acres were devoted to raising produce within the commune. Called *Gardeschwestre* (garden sisters), the women who comprised the garden staff generally worked from 7:30 A.M. until 4:00 P.M. at the direction of the *Gardebaas*.
They had time off for lunch and for snacks mid-morning and mid-afternoon.
If one of the garden sisters had pressing business elsewhere for the day, the
Gardebaas excused her. All the garden sisters were excused from duty on
very hot summer days, but they might also be asked to work late during the
busiest times of the gardening season.

Plowing and raking a kitchen garden in early spring.

Produce was not only grown in large quantities but also in great variety. Following is a list of varieties grown, how the *Gardeschwestre* grew them, how the kitchens prepared them, and whether they were stored or preserved. Information about growing, preparing, and storing all vegetables listed here is courtesy of the State Historical Society of Iowa. Chapter 4 will detail varieties in this listing that are included in our modern seed bank.

🐖 ASPARAGUS (*Sparchel*)
Planted in large beds, asparagus shoots were harvested until early June. They were served cooked and creamed, fresh from the garden. No attempt was made to store or preserve them.

🐖 BEANS (*Schtangebohne*)
String beans were planted around poles, other varieties in rows. Included were yellow beans, navy beans, and lima beans. Excess string beans and yellow beans were either blanched and dried, canned, or pickled for winter use.

🐖 CABBAGE (*Kraut*)
Sown in cold frames, cabbage plants were set out in rows, harvested by the wagonful, shredded, and fermented to create sauerkraut. Surplus sauerkraut was shipped to markets in Chicago. Full heads of cabbage were

stored in earthen basements in the kitchen houses for winter use. Heads
stored with roots intact were replanted in the spring to produce seed.

☛ CARROTS (*Gellweriewe*)

Sown in rows, carrots were harvested in the fall. Some were left in the
ground to go to seed the second year. They were eaten raw, cooked, or
pickled. Whole carrots were also stored in basements for winter use.

☛ CAULIFLOWER (*Bluhmekohl*)

Like cabbage, cauliflower was sown by the *Gardeschwestre* in cold frames
and then set out in rows. They sowed a fall crop in late summer and harvested it in late fall. The plant's large leaves were tied over the heads to
prevent bitterness. Kitchens served the cauliflower cooked and creamed.
Occasionally it was canned or pickled for winter consumption.

☛ CELERIAC (*Knolletsellerie*)

Celeriac is a type of celery with a bulbous root. Sown in cold frames, it was
set out in rows. Kitchens used the bulbs extensively in soups. The stalks, as
such, were inedible, but would occasionally be chopped finely and used as
flavoring. Bulbs were stored in kitchen basements. Some were reserved for
replanting in spring in order to produce seed.

☛ CELERY (*Cellerie*)

Sown in cold frames, regular celery was set out in rows. The stalks needed
to be shaded with boards, newspaper, or wet sheets to blanch them and
prevent a bitter taste. Some whole plants were also stored in basements.
Celery stalks were used much the same way as celeriac bulbs.

☛ CHIVES (*Schnittlauch*)

Gardeschwestre planted clumps of chives in beds and propagated them by
division. Kitchens chopped the leaves and used them to flavor a number
of different dishes. There was no attempt to store or preserve chives.

☛ CITRON MELON (*Tsitter*)

Citron was sown in hills after the danger of frost had passed. It was unpalatable raw. The flesh was cut into slivers or chunks and pickled.

☛ CORN (*Korn*)

Sweet corn was planted in rows in fields and treated the same as the field
corn reserved for animals. It was cooked and the kernels cut from the cob.

Like other vegetables, it was most likely served creamed. No evidence of pickling or other methods of winter storage could be found.

☛ CUCUMBERS (*Gummre*)

Planted in hills after danger of frost, cucumbers were eaten as a salad or pickled in large crocks for winter consumption.

☛ DANDELION (*Zichorie*)

Dandelion provided early spring greens, and *Gardeschwestre* foraged it in the wild. On occasion they also raised it in their gardens and blanched it like celery to prevent bitterness. Kitchens served it as a salad with creamy dressing and often with chopped boiled egg or crumpled fried bacon. *Zichorie* was not consumed during the winter.

☛ DILL (*Dill*)

Dill was sown in beds, and some of it was allowed to reseed to produce a second crop. Kitchens used it primarily to flavor pickled beans and cucumbers, although some dried seed was stored and used to flavor other vegetable dishes.

☛ ENDIVE (*Endiffie*)

Endive is a member of the lettuce family. Sown either in beds or in rows, it was blanched by the garden staff like celery when it began to mature. Kitchens used it primarily in salads. No evidence that it was stored or preserved could be found.

☛ GROUND CHERRY (*Kapsultomettes*)

Ground cherries don't grow on trees and are actually a relative of the tomatillo. They're grown in beds or rows and reseed prolifically. The fruit grows inside a green husk which turns a tan color when the yellow fruit inside is ripe. Kitchens used it in pies and preserved it in jams.

☛ HORSERADISH (*Meerrettich*)

Horseradish generally appeared in gardens in rows and was propagated by rootlets or by replanting roots that had spent the winter in kitchen basements. Mature roots not saved for replanting were scraped and ground into a condiment for meat or chopped, cooked, and creamed as a vegetable. The roots were harvested in fall and stored in basements.

🐛 KALE (*Grienkohl*)
Sown in cold frames, kale was set out in rows by the garden staff. Kitchens cooked and creamed the fresh leaves, but some were also dried and reconstituted for use in winter months. Any surplus served as greens for the kitchen house chickens.

🐛 KOHLRABI (*Kohlrawe*)
Gardeschwestre started kohlrabi in cold frames and later set the plants out in rows. A second sowing in summer produced a fall crop. Kitchen staff peeled and sliced the bulbous stem and served it cooked and creamed. The fall crop was stored in basements for winter use.

🐛 LETTUCE (*Schnittsalaat*)
Sown directly into beds, this loose-head lettuce was served as a salad with creamy dressing and chopped boiled egg. It was commonly known as *Eiersalaat* (egg lettuce). Sometimes lettuce plants were allowed to reseed.

🐛 ONIONS (*Tswiwel*)
Onion seed and onion sets were planted in rows and raised in large fields. Growing onions is a three-step process. Mature onions are planted to produce seed. The seed is sown the next year to produce sets. The sets are harvested in the fall and planted the next year to produce mature onions. All three stages existed in the gardens at the same time. Onions were used in cooking customary vegetable and meat dishes. Mature onions were bundled and stored in basements.

🐛 PEAS (*Erbse*)
Sown in rows, peas were creamed when served fresh. Some were also dried for winter use.

🐛 POTATOES (*Kardoffel*)
The garden staff, often with additional help, cut potato "eyes" from mature potatoes and planted them in rows in large fields. They were plowed out in fall and stored in the church basement. In some form or another, they were served daily at each of the three main meals. Some potatoes were reserved for the next spring's planting stock.

🐦 PUMPKINS AND SQUASH (known collectively as *Kirwiss*)

Sown in hills after the danger of frost, pumpkins and winter squash were harvested in the fall and used in pies or as a vegetable. They were stored in kitchen basements.

🐦 RADISHES (*Rettich*)

Radishes were sown either in rows or in beds. Specimens reserved for seed were transplanted to another area of the garden and allowed to go to seed. Fresh radishes were served as a salad or eaten raw. Sowings were made in the spring and in the fall. Sometimes radishes were allowed to reseed in the fall. The fall crop was stored in basements for winter use. A variety called *Vielfarwige Rettich* (multicolored radish) was an excellent winter keeper.

🐦 SALSIFY (*Schwartswortsel*)

Salsify was a root crop sown in rows. Garden staff dug some of the one-foot to two-foot-long roots in the fall, and kitchens scraped, chopped, and served it as a creamed vegetable. Others were stored in basements for winter use. Still others were left in the ground over winter to produce seed the second year.

🐦 SPINACH (*Spinat*)

Spinach grew in beds. Kitchens cooked it, then ground it up and served it with the addition of beef stock and onion. The staff also blanched some of the harvest in hot water and hung it to dry in kitchen attics for winter use.

🐦 TOMATOES (*Tommetes*)

Sown in cold frames and set out in rows, tomatoes were eaten fresh, canned, or made into ketchup. The best-looking specimens were saved for harvesting next year's seed.

🐦 TURNIPS (*Weissriewe*)

Turnips were sown in rows in August. They were served cooked and creamed, with some being stored for winter use and others saved for spring planting to produce seed.

To a lesser degree, beets, garlic, leeks, peppers, and savoy cabbage appeared in some gardens. The Amana Society also raised onions (seed, sets, and bulbs) and potatoes in very large quantities as cash crops and sold them on the market, generally in the Chicago area. Schoolchildren were recruited to help with the harvest. These crops, along with sweet corn, were grown and harvested under the guidance of the village farm manager (*Farm Mennetscher*) and his crew.

Gardeners often allowed lettuce and radishes to reseed and produce a second crop. Radishes were especially valuable in that regard, as the variety *Vielfarbige Rettich* (multicolored radishes) was an excellent winter keeper when harvested in late fall.

Along with growing and harvesting crops, the *Gardebaas* was responsible for saving seeds from each crop and scheduling its planting during the next growing season. She kept a planting schedule in a gardening journal that helped her choreograph the seasonal dance that assured a bountiful harvest.

Rectangular cold frames in the garden plots made early sowings possible. Sections of wood planks approximately one foot high and usually about 12 feet long comprised the frames. Since wooden storm windows were used as frame covers, carpenters built the frames to accommodate them. The windows measured approximately 28 inches by 58 inches and were placed on the frames in mid February so that the soil would thaw out and dry a bit if wet. Once the soil could be worked, the *Gardebaas* and her staff added well-rotted manure, then raked and leveled the soil to get it ready for sowing. They sowed the seeds in marked rows. Old carpeting was draped over the windows on particularly cold nights to keep heat from escaping. When the weather was warm, a block of wood or a brick served to prop the window covers open for ventilation.

Once the weather warmed to the point where planting in the garden proper could begin, the farm crews fertilized the plots with manure from the village stables and barnyards, tilled them with a horse-drawn plow, and raked them smooth. The garden sisters trampled paths into the soil with their feet and prepared rows for sowing and planting. Both of these activities employed string stretched taut as a guideline, so that the rows and pathways would be perfectly straight, a testimony to the German penchant for *Ordnung* (orderliness).

These string line makers came in two parts. One part was simply a metal or wood stake with a string end tied to it. The other part consisted of a rotatable metal or wood string holder around which the rest of the string was wound. Stuck through the middle of the holder was a second stake. This stake allowed the holder to revolve around it, so that the string could be

A farm worker makes furrows for planting in a kitchen garden.
Note the string guide to the right of the closest furrow.

wound and unwound. The single stake with one end of the string tied to
it was pushed into the ground. Using both hands to hold the stake with the
revolving holder in a horizontal position, the gardener walked away from
the stake in the ground, allowing the holder to unwind the string. When the
gardener came to the spot where the other end of the string end was to be
placed, she eyed the length of the string carefully to make sure it was straight
and then simply pushed the second stake, holder and all, into the ground as
far as the holder would allow. The village blacksmith fabricated most of these
line makers.

During this early part of the gardening season, the *Gardebaas* consulted her garden journal for the planting schedule and studied her notes about how things went the previous year and what might be done differently this year. Then there were the *Drei Kalte Männer* (three cold men) to consider during the first half of May. They represented the ever-present danger that plants especially susceptible to frost damage could be harmed by a succession of three nights of frosty weather. She also consulted the *Farmer's Almanac* as a guide to weather expectations, but she relied primarily on her memory and her cumulative journal notes from prior years. Phases of the moon guided her as she developed her planting schedule. When the moon began waxing after the new moon phase, it was time to plant vegetables that grow above ground. She started plants that bear below ground when the full moon was waning. When the moon was dark, she refrained from planting anything. A good-natured rivalry among the *Gardebaase* of the villages regarding who tended the best garden, grew the most of a given variety, or had the nicest and largest specimens, kept her on her toes.

A good portion of the *Gardebaas'* seed was homegrown. Among the seeds she raised and saved were bean, dill, ground cherry, lettuce, onion, radish, salsify, and tomato. The garden staff generally processed and stored the seeds during the winter when there was more time to do so. Some of the vegetable seed represented varieties that Inspirationists brought with them from Germany to Ebenezer. It's very likely that the *Gardebaas* selected and propagated superior genetic variations in these seeds, both in Ebenezer and later in the Amanas. (My wife Wilma and I still grow some of these heirloom varieties in our vegetable garden. In the 1980s, we founded a seed bank to preserve them for future generations. For more on the seed bank and the varieties included, see chapter 4.)

After the cold frames were prepared, the *Gardebaas* and her helpers planted them with seeds of lettuce, radish, cabbage, and other cole varieties. Another friendly rivalry among the *Gardebaase* involved a contest to see who could produce lettuce large enough for harvest by Easter. The tradition of striving for an Easter harvest still lingers in my family.

Not only cold frames, but smaller boxes placed in window wells or on sheltered porches harbored the first seedlings of the season. Mature cabbage plants stored in the dirt floors of the kitchen house basements over winter saw their first light of spring when the *Gardeschwestre* transplanted them back to the kitchen gardens and carefully tended them to produce seed. Some of that seed was sown immediately for the cabbage harvest in fall and some was kept for sowing the following spring.

Huge quantities of seed potatoes and onion sets went into the ground as well. Both were planted in large plots, usually outside the kitchen garden proper. Seed potatoes were more labor intensive than the onion sets. Gardeners and other villagers recruited for the job cut the larger potatoes into chunks about two inches square, containing at least one or two eyes or buds. Smaller potatoes were planted whole.

Not all of the greens for the communal kitchens came from kitchen gardens. Early in the season, oftentimes even before the Easter lettuce, tender young dandelion greens were gathered from the surrounding countryside. It should be noted, though, that many *Gardebaase* planted cold frames in their gardens with dandelions. They were covered in spring with old carpet runners or straw to produce blanched leaves that were more mildly flavored and could be harvested over a longer time period than those in their natural habitats, where the leaves soon developed a bitter flavor as they aged. Stinging nettle and lamb's quarters were also collected in the wild and prepared much like cooked spinach.

Time spent in the kitchen gardens increased as crops grew and began to bear. The *Gardeschwestre* spread straw among the plants in an effort to keep as many weeds as possible out and moisture in. They used no pesticides. Workers sprinkled ashes on cucumber and squash plants to discourage bugs, cabbages were sprinkled with salt water to kill the larvae of cabbage moths, and some insects were simply plucked from their host plants. Marigolds were often planted between rows of crops to repel bugs, and rudimentary scarecrows discouraged birds.

In addition to the ongoing weeding and watering, harvesting required extra effort and perhaps an extended workday. Produce was gathered by the bushel-basket-full and taken to the kitchen house for processing. Before the advent of plumbing, watering was accomplished with tank wagons and sprinkling cans.

Each kitchen garden had a small, one-room building called a *Gardeheisel*. It served as a storage shed for garden equipment, a place for a brief respite from the hot summer sun, and as a break room with table and chairs where the *Gardeschwestre* ate their mid-morning and mid-afternoon snacks.

Gardeschwestre take a break at the *Gardeheisel*. Young children were sometimes allowed to accompany their mothers or other close relatives.

Tools included the usual hoes, rakes, shovels, and pitch forks; three-pronged cultivators with a long handle, often fabricated by the village blacksmith; and dibbles for planting out seedlings. There were larger cultivators, also made by the blacksmith, with big wheels and waist-high handles that garden workers could push along in front of them between the rows of plants. The *Schubkarre* (wheelbarrow), compliments of the local carpenters, was indispensable. Buckets, watering cans, and baskets made by the village cooper, tinsmith, or weaver, respectively, also found a home here. The gardeners took pride in their work and in their tools. Every day at quitting time the *Gardeschwestre* carefully cleaned all the tools used that day, and those that needed it were kept well oiled.

Amana gardening also encompassed fruit production. Each village had an orchard or two, tended by a knowledgeable orchardist and usually located somewhere along the outer boundaries of the village. Although no pesticides were used in communal kitchen gardens, orchards were an exception. Copper-sulfate-based spray was applied to fruit trees several times during the season.

Spraying apple trees in a village orchard.

In addition to the ground cherries already mentioned, the Inspirationists grew apples, pears, plums, cherries, grapes, raspberries, strawberries, rhubarb, currants, and, in some instances, gooseberries. Schoolchildren helped with the fruit harvest, most often picking and transporting apples from the apple orchards to their storage areas in the village.

Grapes and rhubarb were grown not only for delicious pies and other fruit dishes, but for the wine they produced. Grapes were planted in vineyards and under trellises attached to residences and kitchen houses. In the spring, the men of each village pruned the vines and secured them with supple willow twigs, continuing to care for them all season under the watchful eye of the village vintner. Each able-bodied man cared for about two dozen vines in the vineyards. Occupants of buildings with grape trellises cared for those grapes, most of which ended up at kitchen houses, where they became jam, juice, or pie.

Grapes from the vineyards were reserved for winemaking. During the harvest, school and regular work came to a halt, as all able-bodied villagers were needed for the winemaking effort. Under the direction of the vintner, workers cut bunches and tossed them into willow baskets. The filled baskets

Schoolchildren help with the apple harvest.

were hauled to the press house, often located either in close proximity to the church meeting house or the general store, both of which had deep, cool basements. As the grapes were pressed, the juice ran into a pipeline directly to the designated basement, where the winemaking process continued. A predetermined allotment of properly aged wine was doled out to villagers via wine cards that were punched each time a member came to retrieve a fresh container full of wine. Adult men were allotted one gallon per month and adult women half a gallon.

A rather unusual wine, popular in communal Amana and a hit with tourists still today, is made from the fermented juice of rhubarb stems. It also has an unusual Amana German name: *Piestengel*, hybrid of the English *pie* and the German *Stengel*, meaning "stalk." As the name implies, rhubarb was used in pies as well. The variety grown in Old Amana produced a very large plant, up to five feet tall, with leaves up to 20 inches wide. A specially built device

Communal drying house.

crushed the stalks and drained the juice into receptacles. The resulting wine
was stored and aged alongside the grape wine.

Drying fruit—and some vegetables as well—was essential to assure an
adequate food supply through the winter. Varieties of apples and pears were
the most commonly dried items along with beans, kale, and spinach. Most
villages had special brick drying houses with wooden racks inside. These
houses were quite small, some standing only about five feet tall. There was
a firebox, separated from the drying chamber, and a chimney to vent the
smoke. The woolen mills in Amana and Middle Amana had kilns, so food
to be dried was sent there instead. After drying, the food was stored in linen
sacks, either in kitchen attics or in the kitchen pantry.

Produce was prepared for storage in other ways, too. Freshly picked apples
and pears were wrapped in paper and stored in kitchen basements to give
them a longer life. Prepared dill beans and sauerkraut were stored in barrels or crocks, and many fruits and vegetables were canned. Root crops were
stored in basements as well, either in sand or directly in the dirt floor.

Residents of the Amanas didn't consume all produce grown. All seven
villages raised cabbage, onions, and potatoes on a grand scale. Their sale at
harvest time was an important source of income for the commune.

Processing cabbage for sauerkraut.

The cabbage harvest began with the *Gardebaas* informing the *Kichebaas* that the cabbage was ready. When the word came, all kitchen hands were recruited to help, along with other women from the village. Wagons hauled huge baskets of cabbage to the kitchens where cabbage heads were cleaned, cored, and shredded. After the turn of the century, a cabbage-shredding machine, invented and built in the Amanas, made the chore much easier. The machine was mounted on a wagon and hauled from kitchen to kitchen. Each village had its own machine. Most of the cabbage was salted and packed into barrels and crocks, where it converted to sauerkraut in about four weeks and then was shipped to markets in Chicago. A requisite number of barrels was kept in reserve for use in the kitchens.

In the year 1900, the kitchen house across the street from my ancestral home in Middle Amana produced over 200 gallons of sauerkraut, 165 gallons for sale and an additional 100 gallons for the kitchen house. Multiply that by a similar amount for the other nine kitchens in the village, then by the number of kitchens in the other six villages, and you have an effort of truly epic proportions.

When the time for harvest of mature onions was at hand, the *Farm Mennetscher* sent word to the *Gardebaase*. They, along with other villagers and

Processing eating onions.

Processing onion sets.

older schoolchildren, showed up at the onion fields, usually before daylight, when the weather was somewhat cooler. After the harvest, the onions were cleaned and sorted by size. Most of the largest onions were reserved for packing and shipping to various markets. The remaining onions were stored locally and used in the kitchens. In my native village, the harvest often yielded close to a ton of eating onions.

Onion seed harvests in Middle Amana are thought to have produced about 400 pounds of seed each year. The *Gardebaas* kept a smaller portion of the seed harvest to produce next year's onion sets, but much of it was offered for sale to seed companies. As with mature onions and onion seed, gardeners raised enough sets so that the surplus could be marketed.

The growing and harvesting of onion seed, sets, and eating onions, like the cabbage harvest, was a grand exercise in quality and quantity food production.

Potatoes were raised on large plots of land, usually somewhat larger than those for cabbages and onions. The *Farm Mennetscher* and his staff planted—traditionally on Good Friday—and tended the potatoes. Again, most able-bodied villagers, including schoolchildren, turned out for the potato harvest. Digging potatoes is back-breaking work and, thankfully, was made much easier by a specially designed machine that dug up the potatoes mechanically and tossed them out the back, where villagers collected them in baskets.

Potatoes were then cleaned, sorted by size and quality, and apportioned to the various kitchens. Cooks used the smallest ones right away, and the others were stored in kitchen basements. A portion of the potato harvest was reserved for sale and another portion for seed potatoes the next spring. The total harvest from all the potato fields in the Society could be as much as 40,000 bushels or more.

With the arrival of freezing temperatures, the gardening season came to an end, and gardens and fields were put to bed for the winter. Where plumbing had been installed, water to the gardens was shut off and the lines were drained. Here and there a supplemental dose of manure might be applied to an empty field or garden plot. *Gardeschwestre* oiled and stored the garden tools one last time before the *Gardeheisel* was closed for the season. The *Gardebaas* and the *Gardeschwestre* turned their attention to other needs within the community and in their families. There were clothes to mend, quilts to sew, and items to knit, crochet, tat, or cross-stitch. An artful needle-point creation might appear on a chair seat or on a pillow. Young women

Planting a potato field.

watched and listened closely as the older generation taught them these skills, so that they might master them and one day pass them on to the succeeding generation.

The only touch of green to be found in the Amana landscape as winter set in was in the *Kirchhof* (cemetery) and the *Schulwälder* (school forests). Although evergreen trees aren't strictly utilitarian or a food source, they were an integral part of the landscape in Old Amana. While their greenery was especially appreciated for the fact that it defied the ravages of winter, they were loved for their symbolic and pedagogic value, as well.

Some years after settlement, villagers in the Amanas planted pines and spruces around cemeteries at the village's edge. Evergreens were generally planted within a year or two of the founding of a village, an indication of their importance and veneration. Not only did they define the cemetery borders and provide a bit of green during a rather bleak time of year, they were regarded as symbolic of eternal life.

Inspirationists buried their dead in well-defined rows and in order of death. There were no family plots. Headstones were mostly simple concrete rectangles with a rounded top. On them appeared the name of the deceased, date of death, and age at death. The graves face east, as Inspirationists believe this to be the direction from which Christ will appear at the Second Coming. In communal times, suicide victims were buried in a separate section

A family picnic in the *Schulwald*.

and faced the setting sun in the west. Still today, children and non–Amana Church members are buried in separate sections of the cemeteries.

Through the school forests planted by Amana children, teachers introduced their charges to the concept of planting for the future. Classes in early Amana even got to do their own planting. The results of their labors were the *Schulwälder*, small forests of white pine with a sprinkling of spruce and larch. The pine came from forests near one of the Ebenezer villages. Seedlings from these forests arrived in the late 1850s, and schoolchildren planted groves near Amana, East Amana, and South Amana. As the forests matured, they provided secluded places where children could play, families could have picnics, and lovers could stroll. As we have already seen, the idea of planting for the future was reinforced by including children in the harvest of apples, grapes, potatoes, and onions.

Associated with the planting of evergreens is the "case of the pilfered pines." Oral tradition has it that when the evergreens around the Middle Amana cemetery arrived for planting, there were more seedlings in the shipment than were needed. After the planting was done, some members of the crew took home a surplus seedling or two to plant in their yards. The village elders soon got wind of this transgression and ordered the trees removed. Not wanting to be wasteful, they agreed to plant the trees in the woods

northwest of town. This small evergreen patch in the hardwood forest survives to this day.

Aside from evergreens, one could encounter the occasional deciduous
non-fruit-bearing tree in every village. In many instances these trees were
oaks, some of which were in existence when the Society purchased the land.
Cottonwoods, Osage orange trees, maples, and willows found a home in communal Amana, too. Willows were especially welcome, since they furnished
the raw material for basket making.

Given an inspired message from the commune's first and only female elder
and *Werkzeug*, Barbara Heinemann, there must have been a bit too much sur-
reptitious planting of ornamental trees in the latter years of the 1800s. Her
testimony, printed in the communal *Jahrbuch* (yearbook) for 1880, reads as
follows:

> Wilt thou then prove that it is a beautiful custom to plant trees not bear-
> ing fruit? Know then that the pleasures of the eye and of the flesh and
> the overbearing manner are a mark of worldliness, and that the spirit
> of the world has created in you the desire for such a beginning. Alas,
> away with the idolatry! See ye to it then that all trees not bearing fruit
> be removed from the house, for they belong to the pleasure of the eye.
> You indeed have the opportunity to plant a fruit tree instead, in which
> the Lord and all sensible people take pleasure.

For whatever reason, flower gardens seem to have escaped Sister Heinemann's wrath.

It's important to note that gardening wasn't limited to village kitchen gardens and orchards. Yards were filled with fruit trees, trellises bearing grape
vines, currant and gooseberry bushes, strawberry beds, and here and there a
vegetable variety or two. A striking aspect of photographs showing the yards
of old Amana houses is the fact that there are no lawns. We know how these
yards looked, thanks primarily to intrepid Inspirationist photographers, who
defied an edict against photography as a violation of the Second Command-
ment: "Thou shalt not make unto thee any graven image, or any likeness of
any thing that is in heaven above, or that is in the earth beneath, or that is in
the water under the earth."

If you were to sift through the treasure trove of communal Amana pho-

A communal Amana front yard in Homestead.

tographs housed in the library of the Amana Heritage Society, you would soon encounter an ornamental flowering plant or two growing in front yards. As we have seen, growing plants for ornament rather than for utility was a practice that crept into Amana gardening thanks mainly to Joseph Prestele while he resided in Ebenezer.

Potential sources for decorative plants in Old Amana, aside from those that Prestele grew in his botanical garden, were numerous. One source was the wooded bluffs on either side of the Iowa River. Native ferns, bluebells, columbine, Dutchman's-breeches, even a lady's slipper orchid or two found their way into home gardens. A widespread practice during this era was that of planting woodland ferns along the foundation on the north side of residences. Some of these fern plantings still exist today, our gardens included among them.

Pass-along plants such as peonies, garden phlox, hollyhocks, irises, and daisies followed. This was especially the case during the 1920s, when visitors to the Amanas broke the commune's invisible barrier of social isolation.

Members struck up friendships with outsiders, providing a new and more varied source of decorative plants. These varieties were subsequently passed along from garden to garden among the Society's populace.

Of particular interest for their history and beauty are three blooming plants: the fern leaf peony, the clove currant vine, and the lotus lily.

Peonies were a particularly popular pass-along, not only because they're beautiful in bloom, but also because they're extremely tough and long-lived. Of particular note among these peonies is an early red one called fern leaf peony. Its leaves are unique to the peony world, as its name implies. Somewhat rare, this peony currently sells for an incredible $30 to $60 a pot at nurseries and garden centers. Amana gardeners don't have to pay those prices. While most peony lovers salivate at the thought of owning just one plant, fern leaf peonies grow in profusion here. There have been literally rows of them lining driveways. In fact, it probably wouldn't be much of a stretch to designate the Amanas as the fern leaf peony capitol of Iowa, if not the entire United States.

It all started with Henry Field, a well-known master gardener and nurseryman in the late 1800s, who still lends his name today to the Henry Field mail order nursery business now owned by Scarlet Tanager Holdings. Field had an affinity for fern leaf peonies but found them much too difficult to propagate for his nursery business. He and his family grew them, however, including his sister, a Mrs. Horner. She lived on a farm in rural Homestead, and her family doctor was Dr. William Moershel, an Inspirationist who had a practice in Homestead. At some point during this doctor/patient relationship, Mrs. Horner gifted Dr. Moershel and his wife with several fern leaf peony plants. The plants, having multiplied considerably in the meantime, were inherited by the late Dr. Henry Moershel (William Moershel's son) and his wife, Henrietta, who passed starts along to her Amana friends. The Moershels' daughter, Connie Zuber, has continued the pass-along tradition. Over the decades, the peonies have found their way to all seven villages. Judging by the number of blooms in Homestead every spring, that village continues to be the undisputed champion fern leaf peony grower among the seven villages.

On a typical Prestele trellis, also in the village of Homestead, grows a real rarity: the clove currant vine. Not only is it the only specimen left in Amana gardens, it appears to me quite likely that it's the only one known to exist in the entire United States. How it came to appear in Amana gardens is anyone's guess. Mine would be that it was brought from Germany to Ebenezer and eventually to Amana by Inspirationist immigrants.

The vine is still known to European gardeners today. In the course of my correspondence with a gardener in the Netherlands, he confirmed that it still grows in European gardens, including his own. In the past, clove currant vines grew in European vineyards and were used to flavor wines. The vines become woody with age and, like grapes, can be trained to grow horizontally along wires. When grown on a trellis, as they are in Europe and Amana today, the vines can reach 10 to 12 feet and may need to be tied to the trellis occasionally. Unlike grapes, the vines don't have tendrils with which to attach themselves to a support.

As its name implies, the blossoms on the vines are clove-scented. They appear in early spring and provide a welcome splash of sunny yellow in the garden in addition to their wonderful fragrance. The green, berry-like fruit ripens to black in late summer. It's best used in pies, jams, and jellies.

Those who are familiar with currants know that they grow on bushes and bear clusters of red, white, or black berries. The only discernible difference between vining and non-vining clove currants is that one vines and the other has a typical bushy habit. In all other aspects, these two varieties appear to be identical (see photo 1 in color section).

If I were to choose a single flowering plant that has had the greatest impact on the Amanas, it would certainly be the lotus lily. Eight miles northeast of my South Amana, Iowa, home—between the villages of Middle Amana and Amana proper—lies the Lily Lake, a 170-acre lake whose surface during the growing season is decked out with the stunning beauty of lotus lilies. When they are in bloom, the intoxicating fragrance of these ivory-colored chalices wafts to shore on the wings of midsummer breezes. Like the fern leaf peony, the lotus is a flower introduced into the Amana culture by outside influences. Unlike the peony, however, no one knows from whence it came.

We do know that the lake in which it grows today wasn't present when the Inspirationists moved to Iowa. In 1843, surveyor J. E. Whitcher described a marshland in the approximate location where the lake later appeared. He was surveying the land for the U.S. government so that it could be sold to settlers. It wasn't until 1855 that mention of the marshland appeared again in recorded history. In that year, early Amana settlers described the marsh as a place suited only for cutting hay.

What happened next isn't clear. We do know that in 1865 the Amana settlers set about building the seven-mile-long canal mentioned earlier and known locally as the race or the millrace. Its primary purpose was to divert water from the Iowa River to provide power to woolen mills in Middle Amana and Main Amana, and its course ran in close proximity to the south end of the marshland.

Somehow water from the canal entered the marshland and formed the present-day lake. What historical records don't tell us is whether this occurred as a purposeful act or whether it was an accident. Some oral histories suggest that it was a leaky dike along the canal, but others say that the connection was intentional. Its purpose, the story goes, was to create a reservoir that the canal could draw from when the water in the river was low. The first reference to the lake appeared in the 1874 plat book for Iowa County. It showed the canal running directly into the lake.

Not until the turn of the century do we find the lilies mentioned in print. Unfortunately, there is no reference to their source. We do know that the lake was, and still is, a perfect habitat for this particular American lotus species. It's only two to three feet deep, with a bed of highly fertile, oozing muck.

Two decades after this reference to the lake, we find it brimming with lilies. So spectacular was their bloom that visitors from towns and villages in the region flocked to the lake to see their beauty and to breathe in their delicate fragrance.

The exquisite beauty of the Amana lotus lily makes it easy to understand why it still draws visitors to the Lily Lake every July (see photo 2 in color section).

Much to the consternation of the Amana elders, community youngsters waded into the lake—often sinking more than a foot into the muck—to gather bouquets to sell to this unprecedented influx of outsiders. The elders viewed the lilies as a curse, causing a breach in the isolation from the outside world that they had tended to so earnestly in the past. Even worse, selling the bouquets provided pocket money that no member of the commune was supposed to have.

A pronouncement by the elders soon followed. The lake would be drained, and the offending lilies would be removed. Upon learning of this, the Iowa Academy of Science formed a committee and traveled to Amana to see for themselves what was going on. The elders told them that visitors were trespassing—trampling plowed fields and cutting fences. Even worse, the Sabbath was being defiled, they said, because visitors were disturbing the usual peace and quiet reserved for this day. Worst of all, some enterprising folk even set up stands and sold refreshments along the highway that skirts the lake.

Quite unexpectedly, the Academy of Science delegation convinced the elders that the lake should remain, provided that visitors respect the desire for peace and quiet on Sundays. They did not, but the historical record gives no clues as to why the elders decided to tolerate the intrusion. Part of the reason may have been that the lilies generally bloomed from the end of July until mid August, so the intrusion only lasted several weeks. Media reports during the 1920s estimated that on a busy Sunday during lily season, as many as 1,500 visitors came to the Lily Lake.

So where did the lilies come from? The best guess, in my opinion, is that they were planted by the Meskwaki tribe that lived upriver from the Amana villages. These Native Americans were frequent and welcome visitors, coming to the Amanas to trade goods, hunt game, conduct ceremonies in sacred areas along the Iowa River, and harvest the lotus tubers in the Lily Lake. It's well known that Native Americans occasionally planted lotus tubers in wetlands containing shallow bodies of water. Auburn University's Lotus Project initiated in 1999 reports that

> American Indian tribes treated their native Lotus as a sacred plant with mystical powers and the Comanche, Dakota, Huron, Meskwaki, Ojibwa, Omaha, and Potawatomi used various parts of the Lotus plant as a source of supplemental food.

The Meskwaki tribe, now settled near Tama, Iowa, frequented Amana land before and after it was settled by the Inspirationists. The women harvested tubers in the fall and strung them up to dry for winter use as a food source. Lotus seeds were gathered, roasted, and eaten as well.

Today, the Meskwaki no longer harvest the tubers and seeds, and the Amana commune no longer exists. The lilies, however, are still so numerous that it's impossible to operate a boat on the lake once the pads and flowers have emerged. If you ever find yourself in Iowa during lotus season, I encourage you to make an effort to visit the Lily Lake in Amana. You'll not regret it. A lake covered with so many lotus lilies that you cannot see the water is an exquisite sight. And, as I mentioned earlier, the fragrance will take your breath away.

One aspect of the home garden that we haven't yet addressed is its hardscape, those elements in a garden or landscape that are inanimate. In communal Amana, these elements included primarily wooden objects such as fences, trellises, arbors, benches, swings, and birdhouses. The *Rawatt* and the trellis created by Prestele are included here. Although Prestele constructed his *Rawatt* of wood, some later versions incorporated concrete or stone. Together with the *Rundell*, the *Rawatt* and the trellis added an element to Amana gardens that made them distinctive. The *Rundell* is a raised bed, circular in shape. It was typically constructed of brick or clam shells gathered from the shores of the Iowa River and the millrace.

With the passing of the old order, large-scale vegetable gardening had its last hurrah when the corporate Amana Society decided to continue raising the cash crops—onions, cabbage, and potatoes—that had been so successful in communal days. It rented out the former communal orchards to individuals.

There were other, more pressing endeavors as the new corporation struggled to organize itself as a for-profit entity. Like the Amana garden of Joseph Prestele, the large vegetable gardens and the orchards eventually melted into the soil and were gone. Since around 1980, small orchards have been re-established in South Amana and Homestead. Vegetable gardens still exist, but only in backyards. Their number has declined over the past few decades as our convenience-based society has gravitated to purchasing produce instead of raising it at home. That fact became clear to me and Wilma when we moved back to our ancestral home after an absence of some twenty years.

4

VEGETABLE GARDENING
IN MODERN AMANA

WILMA AND I LIVE in a verdant valley dominated on either side of the beautiful Iowa River by heavily forested bluffs. The soil here is of the type considered to be the richest in the world, found elsewhere only in the Ukraine. We live within the confines of a 26,000-acre game preserve, where deer, ducks, geese, swans, bald eagles, coyotes, foxes, raccoons, the occasional cougar and bobcat, and countless other animal species make their homes amid abundant supplies of food and water. Also located within this preserve are several areas considered sacred by Native Americans in the region. Evidence of their ancestors, in the form of projectile points, spears, pottery, and beads, is offered up by the soil along streams and in plowed fields.

Visitors to South Amana often comment on the beauty of our village and the surrounding countryside. South Amana, known for its beautiful gardens, was—in its horticultural heyday—named the third most beautiful community in the state by the Keep Iowa Beautiful Foundation, an affiliate of Keep America Beautiful, Inc. The other six villages of our former communal society feel a bit slighted by this honor, and rightly so, since they all have a charm and beauty of their own.

Soon after Wilma and I returned to South Amana, we noticed that those wonderful vegetables once grown in magnificent kitchen gardens in communal Amana now appeared chiefly in the home gardens of elderly women. Once the women were gone, those varieties would die with them. We made it our goal to collect seed from the vegetables still surviving and to establish a seed bank to perpetuate them. The women we approached were enthusiastic about our efforts and were only too happy to share their seeds with us. We have been operating our seed bank since 1986 under the aegis of the award-winning Amana Heritage Society, an organization dedicated to the preservation and interpretation of the communal culture and its many artifacts.

Wilma and I grow and bank the precious Amana heirloom varieties listed on the following pages. We make them available to local gardeners, who get preference, and then to all gardeners on a first-come first-served basis. Each vegetable variety has qualities that make it especially desirable. That's why Amana gardeners originally grew it in their kitchen gardens. Look for recipes incorporating some of these varieties in chapter 7.

Each vegetable variety requires a different method of seed collection and processing. Lettuce seed, for example, is ready for processing once the plant has bolted and the seed stalks and heads have turned a grayish tan. In order to release the seed from within the seed heads, we hold each head over a shallow bowl and roll it between our thumbs and forefingers. The released seed drops into the bowl, along with some of the chaff. Once we've processed all the seed heads, we blow gently into the bowl. The chaff is lighter than the seeds, becoming airborne and flowing up and out of the bowl, leaving the seed behind.

We process our radish seed somewhat differently. We harvest the seed stalks and heads once they have turned a light tan color. Radish seed heads are quite tough and flexible, so they don't break open easily. To release the seed, we've repurposed a specially built device used in communal Amana to shake dirt off freshly harvested onion sets. We spread out an old bed sheet and set the device on it. Wearing gloves, we rub the stalks and seed heads across the hardware cloth built into the device. This separates the heads from the stalks and breaks some of the heads open to release the seed, which falls onto the sheet below. We collect the seed and chaff from the sheet, discarding the larger stem parts that have slipped through the hardware cloth. We discard the stem parts left on top of the cloth as well. Then we repeat the rubbing process, which breaks open those seed heads that are still intact after the first rubbing. We use the same shallow bowl for the released radish seed, blowing the chaff out and leaving the seed behind.

Much simpler to harvest is the seed from our salsify plants. Each two-year-old plant produces a bright yellow flower similar to that of a dandelion, only larger. The seed head also looks like that of a giant dandelion. We simply grab the parachutes on the seed head and pull. When thoroughly ripe, the seeds come off the stalk very easily. If they are thoroughly dry, we can put them di-

The author processing radish seed with the communal
"onion shaker." Courtesy Wilma Rettig.

rectly into their storage containers as we take them from the plants. There is
a caveat, however. Strong wind and goldfinches can easily dislodge the seeds
and carry them away. Installing netting over unripe seed heads handily solves
this problem.

We store most of our seeds in airtight containers in an unheated cottage
on our property. Since we produce new seed each year, we don't have to be
concerned about providing proper longtime storage requirements. As insur-
ance against crop failure, our seeds are on deposit in a long-term storage
facility at the Seed Savers Exchange in Decorah, Iowa.

EGG LETTUCE (*Eiersalaat*)

This unique leaf lettuce variety is known locally as egg lettuce, because
communal kitchens usually served it with chopped hard-boiled egg in the
dressing. The leaves are almost completely yellow in color, very tender,
with a slight buttery flavor and texture. Other qualities include heat
resistance, slowness in bolting, and retarded development of bitterness.

Culture is identical to other lettuce varieties. Plant to the thickness of seed in early spring. Seed may be harvested after the stalks begin to turn brown. Left in the garden over winter, this lettuce will self-sow in the spring.

🌰 MULTICOLORED RADISH OR AMANA RADISH (*Fielfarbicher Rettich*)
Amazing in its variability, the multicolored radish is a fun radish to grow, because the grower never knows with certainty what she or he will be harvesting. Its color ranges from purple to red to white. The size is highly variable as well. Some radishes will be small and round, others of medium size with irregular shapes, and yet others quite large and sometimes carrot-shaped.

Culture is identical to that of other radishes. It can be sown quite early in spring (covered with soil to the thickness of the seed), when nighttime lows still dip slightly below freezing. It goes to seed somewhat more quickly than most varieties. This is actually a plus, because the gardener can sow the ripened seed and get a second crop at the end of the fall season. If left to its own devices, it will self-sow, so that a second harvest in the fall is often possible without any additional effort on the part of the grower. Seed stalks can be harvested when most of the individual seed capsules on the stalk have turned a light tan color.

Storing quality is unsurpassed. Today, in some Amana families, *Viel-farbige* (multicolored) *Rettich* are a New Year's Day tradition. If stored in the crisper drawer of a refrigerator, they'll be as fresh and crisp on that day as they were the day they were harvested. We've been known to dine on fall-harvested radishes in the spring, even when new radishes were ready for harvest.

🌰 GROUND CHERRY (*Kapsultomettes*)
A member of the nightshade family, *Kapsultomettes* (capsule tomato) is a native American variety that volunteers in gardens with such ease that it can quickly become a weed. Amana folks grew it for use in pies and in *Kapsulschilee*, a delicious jam that incorporates fresh lemon peel.

Ground cherry culture is similar to that of tomatoes, except that plants grow fairly close to the ground and don't need staking or caging. Fruit and seed are harvested when the husk (capsule) turns brown and drops to the ground. Some gardeners, including Wilma, enjoy eating the raw fruit, but I find it somewhat less palatable.

☛ AMANA STRING BEAN (*Griene Bohne* or *Schtangebohne*)

Typical of many European varieties, this green string bean is flat, as opposed to its more rounded American counterpart. The flavor is outstanding. Culture is identical to that of other green bean varieties. After the danger of frost has passed, plant seeds in circular fashion around bean poles and cover to the thickness of the seed. Seeds may be harvested in late summer or fall after the pods have lost their green color. Other varieties of green beans should not be grown in the same garden (or should be planted as far away as possible), if seed is to be harvested. Segregating the Amana variety keeps the seed pure so that it doesn't hybridize with other varieties.

☛ CELERIAC OR ROOT CELERY (*Knolletsellerie*)

Celeriac or root celery is still a popular vegetable in Europe and has enjoyed increasing popularity in the United States. It's a celery variety grown not for its stalks but for its bulbous root, which has a mild, pleasing celery flavor and is used raw in salads, cooked in soups, or creamed as a vegetable. The stalks are small, strong-tasting, stringy, and generally unpalatable. If finely chopped, they may be used to flavor soups and other dishes.

Culture is slightly different from regular celery, in that some effort must be put forth in order to harvest a reasonably large bulb in the fall. Plants must be kept well watered, especially during dry summers. Outer stalks are removed periodically in order to encourage large bulb formation. Bulbs store well after harvesting in the fall. Plants usually don't produce seed the first year and aren't winter hardy in the Midwest, so some bulbs must be reserved for planting in the following spring in order to obtain seed.

Sow seed in pots or flats in late winter. Press seed gently into soil. Do not cover. Bottom heat with a heating mat is beneficial. Do not let the growing medium dry out. Plant out in the garden when danger of frost has passed.

☛ EUROPEAN BLACK SALSIFY (*Schwartswortsel*)

Schwartswurtsel (black root) is still a popular vegetable in German gardens today. Amana folks prepared it by scraping the black skin from the root in carrot fashion, then cutting it into bite-size pieces and simmering it in water or stock—perhaps with onions added—the liquid thickening to a sauce before serving. The flavor is unique, mild, and delicious, not at all like the American salsify called oyster root.

As with the other vegetables, the seed is sown in spring and covered
to its thickness. Roots will be ready to harvest in fall before the ground
freezes. At the grower's discretion, roots may be left in the ground to winter
over, providing both seed and a larger root the following year. The seeds
are harvested when a fluffy down appears on the seed head.

CITRON MELON (*Tsitter*)

Looking like miniature watermelons, citrons are bound to disappoint anyone who attempts to eat one raw. The flesh is hard, white, and practically
tasteless. Citrons are eaten primarily in a pickled form, with the dominant
flavoring usually that of cloves and cinnamon. The vines are also quite
similar to watermelon, as is this plant's culture. When processing citron,
save the seeds, dry them, and plant to the thickness of the seed when the
weather turns warm in late May or early June.

EBENEZER ONION (*Tswiwel*)

A popular onion in the Northeast and Upper Midwest because of its winter
keeping qualities, the Ebenezer onion was introduced to the trade by
Inspirationists during their sojourn in the Ebenezer villages in New York.
Oral tradition has it that huge surpluses in the Ebenezer kitchen gardens
resulted in the sale of this onion on the nearby Buffalo market. Its popularity was quickly established because of its superb keeping qualities over
winter. It's occasionally still available through such well-known mail order
firms as Burpee Seeds and Gurney's.

Culture is identical to other varieties. Mature onions planted in spring
produce seed, which is harvested in summer. The following spring, the
seed is planted to its thickness and produces small onions called sets.
These are harvested in late summer and stored in a cool, dark place over
winter. Sets planted the next spring produce mature onions. The mature
onion is yellow, of medium size, and has a fairly mild flavor. Occasionally,
the seed produces a white or red onion.

We garden organically and no-till. Not having to till means that we can
simply walk out to the garden and start planting in the spring. For seeds, we
lay out a row of compost about eight inches wide and four inches deep and
sow them directly into that. We follow the general rule that planting depth
should approximate the thickness of the seed, meaning that larger seeds

such as bean seeds should be planted deeper than the much smaller radish seeds.

Beyond the happy fact that we don't have to till first, the compost rows offer other advantages. They provide the nutrients to give seedlings a good start in life and, since they raise the seedbed above the surrounding soil, they also help with drainage during very wet weather. For plants, we simply dig holes in the existing soil and drop a bit of compost in each one before inserting the plant and backfilling the hole with compost.

When that first spell of warm weather with above-freezing temperatures at night comes along in spring, it's sometimes difficult to resist the temptation to get everything into the ground: plants, seeds, bulbs, rhizomes, and corms. Every year I wrestle with that impulse, especially when spring comes early to our Cottage-in-the-Meadow Gardens, as it has for the past several years.

Many gardeners have their favorite methods for determining when those magic dates for planting finally arrive. In my village, it's traditionally Good Friday for potatoes, a leftover practice from communal times. Plants especially susceptible to frost have to wait until the *Drei Kalte Männer* have made their appearance in May. Specific dates on the calendar are favored by some gardeners as are the various phases of the moon. For the more scientifically minded, a soil thermometer does the trick.

I, on the other hand, prefer to let the plants themselves tell me when it's safe to plant. Here's a list of plants we consult when we begin gardening each year: When forsythia blooms, it's time to plant the seeds of alyssum, carrots, cornflower, peas, poppies, and radishes. When cherry trees and flowering quince bloom, it's time to plant broccoli, cabbage, cauliflower, larkspur, onion, pansy, and snapdragon. When lilacs are in full bloom, it's time to plant the seeds of beans, corn, cucumber, marigolds, morning glory, nasturtium, petunias, squash, sunflower, and zinnias.

When bridal veil (spirea) and wild cherry trees bloom, it's generally safe to assume that the last frost of spring has passed. This is the time to plant all those frost-tender plants you've been eyeing at garden centers for the past month or so.

As I've indicated above, cool-season vegetables—including most salad greens, peas, onions, and popular cole crops such as cabbage, cauliflower, and broccoli—can tolerate temperatures slightly below freezing. Warm-season vegetables such as tomatoes, peppers, eggplant, squash, and melons can suffer if air temperatures drop below 40 degrees, unless you've protected the transplants with cloches or some other device.

A special word of caution about caladiums and peppers: Caladiums are sensitive to temperatures below 50 degrees. Prolonged exposure will cause the leaves to droop, and eventually the plant will go dormant right in the middle of spring. Those beautiful multi-colored leaves look great in stores and greenhouses early in the season, but if you want to keep them looking that way, don't purchase caladiums until the nighttime temperatures are consistently above 50 degrees. Alternatively, you can purchase them early and keep them indoors in a warm, bright spot (no direct sun) until it's safe to plant them outdoors. Peppers also follow the 50-degree rule. Their leaves won't be harmed much by lower temperatures, but they generally will not bloom well, if at all, if it's below 50 degrees when it's time for the plant to start producing flower buds. Hence, there will be few or no peppers.

On the other hand, some amazingly hardy plants can survive even hard frosts in the spring. A number of years ago temperatures plunged into the teens just as tulips and daffodils were about to bloom (some of the earlier varieties already had blossoms), and the garden perennials had poked their heads up about six inches out of the ground. I went to check on them the next morning and found that the tulip leaves had literally turned blue, the daffodil leaves were drooping to the ground, and the perennials were stiff as a board. I tried to bend a phlox shoot and it simply snapped in two. I was convinced that every plant that had dared to venture above ground was doomed. Yet, much to my surprise, two days later there was barely any evidence of frost damage anywhere.

We try to avoid varieties that are prone to insect and disease damage. In the vegetable garden, we generally avoid all deterrents, whether chemical or organic. Instead, we plant much larger quantities than we require, so that even if there is a disease or insect problem we will still be able to harvest enough produce for our needs. If a particular variety makes it through the growing season with little damage, we share the surplus with our neighbors, offer it to local restaurants, or give it to friends to sell at a local farmers market.

In the flower garden, we use insecticidal soap or neem oil to control insect damage. In particularly stubborn cases, where all my prior efforts have failed,

I will resort to a can of Raid house and garden spray. Fortunately, that's a relatively rare event. I use no control at all for diseases. Mildew and black spot are a rare occurrence, because I grow plants that are disease resistant. This is an especially important tactic, because I like densely planted beds that look lush, which is an open invitation to mildew on susceptible plant varieties due to poor air circulation.

1. Clove currant vine in Homestead.

2. The lilies are so numerous that they cover the entire surface of the Lily Lake.

3. Front entry to our home.
(The white bench is quite old, appearing in a photo of Wilma's grandparents on their fiftieth wedding anniversary, March 24, 1946.) Note the Prestele trellis.

4. Weeping mulberry with conical hydrangea blossoms in background left.

5. Lath house interior.

6. South Amana banana canna.

7. As you turn around and face south, the patio area reveals itself. The table and chairs long ago made way for potted plants. Leaves of different sizes, colors, and shapes create interest in this patio vignette. Note the generous use of coleus (between potted maples, at lower left, and at mid left).

8. Potted plants in the cistern area, among them
glory bower and a variegated schefflera.

9. 'Dre's Dagger' fern with crisscrossing leaflets.

10. *Kinderschul* cottage with restored fence. Garden dominated by Ravenna grass.

11. A restful corner in the cottage garden.

12. Hydrangea hedge bordering a large grassy area we jokingly call our meadow.

13. Screen house in the meadow covered with sweet autumn clematis.

14. A portion of our organic vegetable garden.

15. *Gardelaub* in our gardens.

16. 'Harrison's Yellow' rose, the oldest plant in our gardens.

17. Vase Garden with yellow corydalis.

18. One of the lichen-encrusted oak chairs in the Northside Garden.

19. Chinese seven-son flower tree blooms in August. Exfoliating bark, double white fragrant flowers, and red calyces are among its attributes. In the background is a bed laid out in three scallops. The left and right scallops are planted in red salvia and the center scallop in variegated miscanthus grass.

20. This older photo shows the pond as it was before it disappeared behind a clump of burgeoning, variegated miscanthus grass, which is just getting started here (foreground, bottom left). A new planting of 'Gull's Wing' Siberian iris echoes the foliage of the cattails in the pond.

21. (*left*) This fountain in the arbor directly behind the pond discharges water into the pond, from which it is pumped back up to the top of the fountain.

22. (*below*) Flowering spurge takes front and center in one of our cottage garden vignettes.

23. 'Loraine Sunshine' heliopsis dominates this vignette. Notice that its variegated leaves provide interest even when it is not in bloom. Completing the vignette are (from left to right) 'Rozanne' perennial geranium, flowering spurge, and golden tansy.

24. 'Gibraltar' lespedeza with similar hued periwinkle and alyssum.

25. Poppy mallow winds its way through Mexican bamboo.

26. Vining asparagus fern tops an arbor just off the
public walkway that bisects our garden.

27. Perennial sweet pea in our cottage garden.

28. 'Painter's Palette' persicaria.

29. 'Raspberry Blast' supertunia.

30. 'Rozanne' geranium.

31. Unusual rolled petals of 'Henry Eilers' rudbeckia
with dark-leafed castor bean in background.

32. Tree peony 'Shimanishiki'.

33. 'Rob Vanderlinden' tulip with
double-flowered daffodils in background.

34. (*above*) 'John Cabot' rose.

35. (*right*) Yellow corydalis.

36. (*left*) Wilma spoofs Grant Wood's painting, *Woman with Plants*. She's holding a pass-along from the original plant used in the painting.

37. (*below*) Connie Zuber canna.

38. (*above*) Hammered botanical prints.

39. (*right*) Finished della Robbia centerpiece.

40. Finished wreaths.

41. Gnome home at base of tree.

42. No-wa-wa fountain.

43. Tropical garden room views.

FLOWER GARDENING
IN MODERN AMANA

WHAT MODERN AMANA gardens may lack in fruit and vegetable production, they certainly make up for in blooming plants. Tourists visiting the Amanas often mention the beautiful flower gardens they find here.

When I moved to South Amana in 1977, I soon discovered that tourists and locals alike had dubbed the village the flower capital of the Amanas. It wasn't hard to see why. Flowers seemed to blossom forth from every nook and cranny in every yard. There was even some friendly competition among four elderly women who had grown up under the communal system, each of whom gardened in one of the four yards adjoining an intersection. (I dubbed it the *Oma* intersection, *Oma* meaning "grandma" in our German dialect.) Due to their physical location, each gardener could keep a close eye on what the other three gardeners were up to, lest one of them outdo the others. It reminded me of that friendly competition among the old Amana *Gardebaase* mentioned earlier.

The South Amana house I live in has been in Wilma's family since it was built in 1900. From the very beginning, it has housed flower gardeners. My mother-in-law, Carrie Shoup, was no exception, being considered South Amana's gardener extraordinaire and topping even the four women at the *Oma* intersection. After her passing in 1984, Wilma and I became the heirs of her legacy. We have greatly expanded her gardens and acquired an adjoining property, complete with a cottage, which has allowed me to dabble a bit in cottage gardening and also save and restore a historic structure.

Come with me now as I take you on a tour of our Cottage-in-the-Meadow Gardens, elaborate a bit on my gardening philosophy, and introduce you to some of my favorite plants. According to the new USDA zoning map, our gardens are located at the southern edge of zone 5a, where wintertime low temperatures have ranged from −20 to −15 degrees Fahrenheit during the years from 1976 to 2005. Since that time, our wintertime temperatures have been considerably warmer.

Before we start, a word about our name. Wilma and I actually never intended to name our gardens. It all started with a phone call from a gardener who was a member of a garden club in the nearby city of Cedar Rapids. The club wanted to know if they could get together with us to talk about a request from the Smithsonian Institution in Washington, D.C. Mystified, we agreed to a meeting. We learned that the Smithsonian had contacted numerous garden clubs in larger midwestern cities, asking for assistance in identifying gardens of note, particularly those with an interesting history. It seems that the Smithsonian had come under criticism for primarily listing gardens of interest on the East and West Coasts, while almost completely ignoring the Midwest.

As we continued our conversation with the garden club, it soon became apparent that our gardens fit well with the long list of criteria supplied by the Smithsonian. Club members worked tirelessly on documenting and mapping our gardens in preparing the Smithsonian application. One of the items on it asked for the garden's name. Because we have a cottage on our property and because we have for many years jokingly referred to the open, grassy area to the east of it as "the meadow," I suggested "Cottage-in-the-Meadow Gardens." Everyone liked it, including the Smithsonian. The application was approved, and that's how we were accorded the great honor of being listed in the Smithsonian Institution's *Archives of American Gardens*.

Although our gardens are named, they are, at this point, still private. However, we happily give tours to any person or group that requests one. I've taken the liberty of assuming that my readers would like one, so on with the tour.

Our starting point is the main entrance to our gardens at the end of the front driveway, just off the street. Let's take a look, first, at the architecture of the main residence. The trellising on the west and south walls supported grape vines during the communal era. The vines had two purposes. One was obviously to produce grapes for eating, winemaking, pie, and jelly. The second was to keep the house cooler during Iowa's hot summers. As noted earlier, all plantings around residences were supposed to be utilitarian, hence the trellised grapes to the exclusion of other vines.

The house, built in 1900, was the last "old" Amana house in South Amana. Builders used brick almost exclusively in our village because South Amana was one of several villages that had a brickyard. Exterior walls are double; that is, there are two parallel walls of brick with an air space in between, providing very effective insulation. Wilma was born in this house, and it's still in the family after four generations. (See photo 3 in color section.)

The property was also the site of the first structure in South Amana, a log cabin bought from a settler. The cabin, located on the bluffs above the village, was hauled on skids to its new site. It housed the Amana workers as they constructed the village's first buildings. The cabin's fate is unknown, but it had probably been dismantled before the present residence was built.

As you move closer to the house, note, on your left, the unusual leaves of the plant that fills the bed between the driveway and the house's foundation. This is 'Painter's Palette', a tough and hardy plant that's showy but needs little care other than an occasional drink when the ground is really dry.

Now turn to your right and take a look at the garden beds to the right of the driveway that contain more of the 300-plus varieties of plants that flourish in our gardens. The oval bed bordered by large stones contains a weeping mulberry. (See photo 4 in color section.) Fortunately, it doesn't produce berries. If you're familiar with the purple mulberry fruit, you know that it can be quite messy, especially after it has passed through the digestive tract of birds.

The structure closest to the street is a lath house. Its unusual trapezoidal shape was dictated in part by the triangular bed to the left. This bed, which continues along the fence to the east, is historic, so we didn't want to disturb it in any way by building a more conventional structure that would have intruded upon it. Carrie Shoup, Wilma's mother, laid it out in the 1940s. She lined it with rocks she had gathered on vacation trips with her family. Sweet autumn clematis vines adorn the lath house. In the fall, they produce clouds of fragrant white blossoms. Note the bench and "coffee table" inside the lath house. Most plants in here are tropical and must be carried indoors in the fall. (See photo 5 in color section.)

In this general area you'll also find potted cannas, part of a larger canna collection you'll see later on your tour. The bushes on either side of the lath house entrance are 'Limelight' hydrangeas, a new variety from the Netherlands. The hydrangea bushes against the fence are the old-fashioned 'Anna-belle' and were planted in the early 1940s.

Continuing in counterclockwise fashion, we turn next to the area that has a small freestanding trellis with vines on it. Note the very dark-leafed plant at the south end of the trellis. This is a canna 'Australia', a rather rare plant. It's distinguished by the fact that, among dark-leafed cannas, it's the only one that retains its coloration the whole season. Leaves of other dark varieties turn greenish during the summer. At the opposite end of the trellis is another canna. This one is called the banana canna because its large leaves resemble those of a banana plant. (See photo 6 in color section.)

This particular plant has an interesting history. In 1998 we had an unheard-of weather event that had meteorologists puzzled for years. Unfortunately, the residents of South Amana, their houses, and their gardens were subjected to a violent storm that brought sustained straight-line winds of at least 150 miles per hour. The winds lasted a full fifteen minutes. We lost thirteen trees in our gardens and went, in an instant, from being shade gardeners to sun gardeners. Debris around our two-story house was piled so high that the house was not visible from any direction.

In the aftermath of the storm, landscapers had to extract a stump from a large, old maple tree they had dismantled in the front yard (where the ornamental pear tree now stands). They filled in the resulting hole and sowed grass in the new soil. As I watered the sprouting grass, I noticed a seedling that definitely wasn't grass. Curious, I potted it up and was amazed at what resulted: the very banana canna that you see here. Evidently, someone had grown this canna in the soil that the landscapers had brought in. The canna must have produced seeds, one of which actually sprouted in our front yard. Cannas are tropical plants, so I was amazed that the seeds had, in all likelihood, survived an Iowa winter. We regularly burn plant refuse in our vegetable garden at the end of the season, including canna stalks killed by the frost. We now have banana cannas coming up in our vegetable garden every spring, evidently from the seeds that have escaped the flames.

Next we turn our attention to the area under the front porch. Note the fern in one of the hanging baskets. Its name is 'Fluffy Ruffles', a rare fern that I've had for about 25 years. Difficult to reproduce because it's sterile, it is a sport of the common Boston fern.

'Fluffy Ruffles' fern.

As you turn around and face south, you'll discover what's behind the trellis with the vines. This area used to be our front patio, but, as you can see, potted plants have taken over completely. (See photo 7 in color section.)

Here you'll find additional canna varieties in our growing collection as well as lots of coleus plants. Note that very few of these plants bloom. The challenge here was to create lots of color and interest using only leaves. I potted the Japanese maples, instead of planting them in the ground, for two reasons: I'm assured that they'll not suffer any winter damage, and I can move them around to different locations at will. Most of the plants you see in this area will winter either in an unheated room in our basement (where they remain dormant until spring) or under grow lights in our tropical garden on the second floor of our residence. For more on the garden room, see chapter 8.

As you pass through the patio area, take a peek through the door on your left. This was the washhouse under the old Amana communal system. We've converted it into a potting shed/greenhouse. We still use the cistern under the raised area just outside the potting shed door. It collects the rainwater from the roofs of both the main residence and the building outside which you're standing. The water is piped into the basement of our residence, where it's used to water indoor plants, and to the potting shed, where it's used to water not only the plants inside the shed but also most of the plants in pots in all areas of our gardens. At last count, we had over 200 potted plants. All plants in the previous patio photo are potted.

Sitting on top of the cistern are numerous potted tropical plants, including glory bower vine, whose deep scarlet blossoms are surrounded by a contrasting white husk. Here you'll also find a variegated schefflera and a number of different alocasias, including elephant ear, 'Frydek', and 'Hilo Beauty'. (See photo 8 in color section.)

Before you follow the sidewalk as it makes a 90-degree turn to the left, note the fern in the low pot just behind the open book with an inscription on each page. It is a very unusual fern, with the leaflets on its fronds crossing to form an X. (See photo 9 in color section.)

As you round the corner of the potting shed and step out into the open, turn in the direction you just came from and take a look at the vine climbing into the evergreen arborvitae tree. This is a kiwi vine. The fruit is smaller than a kiwi you buy in the store, isn't fuzzy—you can eat it like a plum or a grape—and has a sweeter taste than the commercial varieties. It's green in color and develops a purplish tint when ripe.

Now turn toward the alleyway that divides our property approximately in half. The small brick cottage with fenced-in yard was the daycare center (*Kinderschul*) for children under the old communal system and was constructed in 1869. We restored it some years ago and use it now for storage of tools and other garden-related items. We also restored the fence in recent years. (See photo 10 in color section.)

Continue toward the cottage and walk under its porch. Step to your right out into the fenced cottage garden and note the tall ornamental grass in the center. This is Ravenna grass, the tallest grass (up to fifteen feet) in our zone 5 gardens. In the southwest corner of this garden, you'll find a small, sunken water feature. The container is an old wash kettle that our neighbors removed from their residence during a remodeling project. It contains a water lily and dwarf cattails, as well as several frogs, depending on the season. My father built the bench in the southeast corner in the early 2000s. (See photo 11 in color section.)

Leaving this garden, you'll return to the cottage porch and continue out into the grassy area to the east of the cottage. This is the "meadow" that has become part of our gardens' name.

To your right is a long hedgerow of 'Annabelle' hydrangeas. I created this hedge from the original planting you saw earlier in the front yard of the main residence. (See photo 12 in color section.)

In the southeast corner of the meadow is a trellised screen house that I designed and my father helped build in 1990. Wilma and I relax in the inviting hammock chairs inside when we take a break from our garden labors. We also eat our evening meals in the screen house, weather permitting, and enjoy the beautiful view into the river valley from this vantage point. (See photo 13 in color section.)

As you look into the farm field beyond the pillar-and-trellis rose garden, you'll see the South Amana Cemetery. Note that the headstones are small, white, and identical. As in olden days, there are no family plots. Residents are buried in order of death.

A few steps further to the north is our hundred-year-old vegetable garden. Until recently, it contained an asparagus bed that was part of the original garden and still contained the original planting. Wilma's grandfather collected the plants in the wild and planted them here in the early 1900s. (See photo 14 in color section.)

The easternmost part of the garden is reserved for the seed bank discussed in detail at the beginning of chapter 4. As mentioned and pictured in chapter 4, we have rescued vegetable varieties that Inspirationists brought with them from Germany and raised in their communal kitchen gardens.

As we leave the vegetable garden, we'll head west toward the public walkway. Here, a small orchard contains some unusual varieties. The small tree nearest the vegetable garden is a Mirabelle plum. Amana settlers brought this variety with them from Germany. It's a small, sweet, yellow, freestone plum that is virtually unknown in the United States. It must be propagated by grafting since it doesn't come true to seed. There are very few of these trees left in the Amanas.

The next tree west is an apricot, then comes a Bartlett pear, and last in the row is a shipova. This unusual fruit is a cross between a mountain ash and a pear. The fruit is small, squat, russeted, has a slight red blush, and is quite sweet. This is one of only a handful of shipovas in the United States.

Directly north of the shipova is a Stanley plum, the same plum that's dried to make prunes.

The small apple tree just beyond the plum and beneath the Jonadel apple tree is very special. Jeffrey Meyer, a young Amana man, started a large horticultural business in Jacksonville, Florida. However, his first love is antique fruit varieties. On one of his fruit-scouting trips to Ohio, he came upon a family with a very old apple tree, who clamed that Jonathan Chapman, more popularly known as Johnny Appleseed, planted it. Meyer took some cuttings from the ancient tree and propagated them. This is one of those trees.

As you pass through the arbor and step back onto the walkway, note the structure just ahead of you with the garden swing in it. Amana folks call it a *Gardelaub* (garden arbor). Practically every residence had one of these in the yard during communal times. It was originally covered with trellises and grapevines on all sides. If there were young children in the family, the swing was sometimes removed in favor of a sandbox. Occasionally, there was a second *Gardelaub*, one with a swing and the other with a sandbox. (See photo 15 in color section.)

We'll proceed south on the walkway for a short distance and turn right onto the sidewalk leading to the back entrance of the residence. Note the barrel fountain to your left and the herb garden in front of you. The kitchen is right inside the entrance, so Wilma can come out and, with only a few steps, snip herbs as she cooks. Note also the bed of ivy to the left of the kitchen entrance. I rooted a sprig from Wilma's wedding bouquet, and Wilma's mother planted it in this bed in 1962.

As we continue to our right toward the northeast corner of the residence, you'll see a very tall rosebush, the oldest plant in our gardens. This variety is 'Harrison's Yellow' and has been growing in this spot since the early 1900s. (See photo 16 in color section.)

In the corner to the right is a small bed with a Grecian column and a blue urn, just north of the *Gardelaub*. Note the low-growing, lacy-leafed plant with small yellow flowers. This is yellow corydalis, one of a number of plants brought to this country by plant explorers—botanists who travel the world, often to remote areas, in search of new species or new members of an existing species. I'm in contact with several of these explorers and acquire some of their finds to try out in our gardens. I recommend this plant highly, as it grows happily in almost all garden situations. It may already be available in your local garden center. (See photo 17 in color section.)

We'll follow the cobblestone path to the north side of the residence. This area is home to a collection of hostas, ferns, and fruit trees. Planting ferns along the foundation on the north side of the house is an old communal tradition. These ferns probably date back to the early 1900s. The apple and pear trees among the flower beds echo the utilitarian bent of the old communal leaders. Note the two large, weathered oak chairs. My father built them around the year 2000. (See photo 18 in color section.)

As you come to the end of the cobblestone pathway, you'll find yourself on a small lawn on the street-side of the residence. The tree with the open habit and peeling bark is a Chinese seven-son flower tree. This is a tree that does just about everything a gardener could want. Aside from the interesting patterns its peeling bark creates, it blooms in late summer, when no other trees are in bloom. The blossoms are white, double, and fragrant. True to its name, the blossoms appear in clusters of seven. Once the petals are gone, the sepals (the small structures which hold the petals in place) enlarge and turn a tawny pink. Then the tree blooms pink for several weeks. As if that were not enough, the leaves turn red before they fall. Monarch butterflies flock to the tree in droves when it's in bloom. (See photo 19 in color section.)

Wilma's mother laid out a scallop garden in this area with three contiguous scallops during the 1950s, again with rocks she had collected on vacations. Partially hidden behind the center scallop is a small fishpond installed by Wilma's father in the early 1930s. Water circulates through a fountain inside the white arbor and back into the pond. We grow the red salvias in the two outer scallops in memory of Wilma's mother, who grew them here each year. (See photos 20 and 21 in color section.)

Follow the short flagstone path tucked between the hostas and the salvias, and you'll be back up on the driveway where you started. *Auf Wiedersehen!*

Caring for almost an acre of plants, some two hundred plants in pots, and the hardscape that accompanies them can be a daunting task, despite the fact that I'm retired from an administrative career at the University of Iowa. While Wilma helps me occasionally, and I reciprocate, we essentially take care of our respective domains single-handedly. She does the vegetables, and I do the flowers.

During the growing season, we could easily let gardening rule our lives. We both have part-time jobs for a few hours during the week, are involved in community service, and enjoy visiting with our friends, playing musical instruments, and attending many public events. In order to do all that, I've modified my approach to gardening. I mulch all flower beds, which reduces the need for weeding and watering considerably. And, for the most part, I grow plants that require little or no coddling. If a plant doesn't perform well on its own, it usually ends up on the compost heap.

Perhaps, in revealing my inclination not to spend time nursing ailing plants, I risk being labeled a male reincarnation of the feisty Thalassa Cruso. You may remember Thalassa from her appearances on talk shows in the 1960s or from her own public television show, *Making Things Grow*, from 1966 to 1969. She unceremoniously grabbed plants and jerked them out of their pots, whacked them mercilessly with a big butcher knife to divide them, and in general treated them in every way but gently. While I love garden-ing and am certainly not a masochistic gardener, I do have to draw the line somewhere if I'm going to have a life outside a collection of gardens the size of ours.

If I had to characterize our gardens succinctly, I would say, "old inter-mingles with new" is one of the strong themes that runs throughout them. Brand new varieties mix with old ones. That's true of both the vegetable gar-den and our flower beds. *Eiersalaat* (our heirloom lettuce) keeps company with the latest cucumber variety, a hundred-year-old rose arches over the newest daylilies and heucheras, ancient grape vines intertwine on the *Garde-laub* with a newly planted wisteria, and rocks we've gathered commingle with the ones my mother-in-law brought home from vacations.

A second theme that I've woven throughout the flower beds involves color. Pinks, purples, and lavenders are set off by yellows and golds. Aiming for an overall feeling of serenity, I've favored pastel shades over deeper tones. One of the great rewards of opening our gardens to visitors is the fact that so many of them remark on the peacefulness and serenity they feel as they move through them. It validates my efforts.

That's not to say that there are no punches of color. The bright red heir-loom salvia beds in the scallop garden facing the street are a literal traffic stopper. The reds, burgundies, and oranges of coleus enliven a collection of potted plants on the front patio. Spring brings the glowing reds and oranges of species tulips and crown imperials. Red Flanders poppies, to which I'll introduce you shortly, mingle with pure white ox eye daisies.

Another unifier is *Hosta undulata* 'Albomarginata'. I've used it as a theme plant and scattered it throughout many of our beds to help tie them together. It's a great hosta to use for that purpose as it can tolerate a few hours of full sun. I especially like the effect of its emerging leaves in the spring before they have completely unfurled. In the dim light of dawn and dusk they glow like luminarias.

While I'm on the subject of hostas, a few words about leafy plants are in order. There are already plenty of challenges facing every gardener, but I like to set special challenges for myself every so often. In recent years, I've begun to focus more on leaves than on flowers. I've been exploring the possibilities for creating interest and beauty with different leaf colors, shapes, sizes, and textures. Perennial beds are especially amenable to such an approach. Since the majority of the perennials we can grow here in our zone 5 gardens flower for relatively short periods of time, leaves can take on a special importance in sustaining color and interest.

A plant must have leaves to survive, but it may not always flower—perhaps most especially not when it's supposed to do so on cue. Plants grown primarily for their interesting leaves are thus more dependable, and the effect you want to create generally lasts the whole season long. Some of the more common and widely available "leaf plants" include coleus, decorative sweet potato vines, ferns, caladiums, lamb's ears, hostas, lamiums, moneyworts, coral bells, and cannas. Gardeners once grew the latter two primarily for their flowers, but a breeding revolution in the last decade has produced many interesting leaf colors and variegations. As with hostas, many gardeners now regularly remove flower stems from these plants in order to draw more attention to the leaves. In the process, it encourages the plant to become more vigorous and thus to put out more leaves.

The undisputed champion in the list is coleus. Coleus has become the hosta of the annual world with an incredible number of varieties. There is so much variation in leaf color, texture, shape, and size that you're bound to find several that will fit into your garden scheme nicely. Colors include pink, green, red, white, yellow, burgundy, bronze, purple, and orange. There are varieties with giant leaves, like the Kong series from Burpee. The average leaf size on our specimen this year was six inches by nine inches! There are also very tall varieties (e.g., 'Big Blonde' at three feet) and varieties that do well in full sun (e.g., 'Pineapple' and 'Sun Power' or any in the solar series).

Coleus is at home growing in the ground, in mixed containers, or all by itself as a specimen. It's not a demanding plant, asking only for well-drained soil, watering when it gets dry, and occasionally a drink of fertilizer if you want a particularly vigorous plant.

Another aspect of my philosophy is that for the most part, I tend to ignore the gospel preached by many gardening professionals. I don't consult the color wheel to make sure that I have the proper combination of colors in a bed, nor do I agree that tall plants must always be consigned to the back of the border. Instead, I plant in vignettes. By this I mean that I tend to plant in groupings that look good together and that have roughly the same growing requirements. A grouping may involve three plants that flower at the same time and present an interesting combination of colors; they may have leaves in different sizes, shapes, textures, and colors; or they may vary in height. The different vignettes in a bed are tied together by sharing some of the same colors.

FAVORITE PLANTS IN
COTTAGE-IN-THE-MEADOW
GARDENS

I'M OFTEN ASKED what my favorite plant is. Invariably, my mind goes blank. There are so many, and I like them all! But one thing I can do with ease is tell you what plants I'm currently using to create my vignettes. Like all gardens, ours are a work in progress, so my vignettes are always evolving. Here are some tried-and-true plants that I use quite often. The last three are historic potted plants that I treasure.

Coleus

(See photo 7 in color section.) As mentioned in chapter 5, coleus is versatile and easy to grow, making it a popular garden staple. It first burst onto the garden scene during the Victorian era, coming originally from Indonesia and Africa where it is native. Dutch traders carried several species to Europe in the mid 1800s, where plant breeders began to hybridize them. Each hybridizer tried to create a new hybrid with leaves more wildly variegated and colored than those created by his or her competitor. New plants often commanded outrageous prices.

In the 1890s, both English and American gardeners adopted coleus with great enthusiasm, and the coleus craze was born. They not only incorporated coleus into their garden beds, but they took cuttings in the fall to use as houseplants during the winter months.

In modern times, the popularity of coleus waxes and wanes. As evidenced by the increasing number of varieties available at garden centers, in mail order catalogs, and online, coleus is once again on the upswing. There are currently an incredible 1,431 named varieties on the market. Many go by such fanciful names as 'Bada Bing', 'Between-the-Lines', 'Careless Love', 'Darth Vader', 'Gatorade Gal', 'Holy Guacamole', 'Nearly Nothin', 'Radical But-terbean', 'Peuce Snit', and 'Religious Radish', my personal favorite, not only because of its beautiful pink, red, and dark maroon colors, but also because my family name means "radish" in German.

Hardiness: grown as an annual in all but zones 10 and 11
Height: 18–24 inches, some varieties even taller
Spread: 9–15 inches
Bloom time: late summer, early fall
Bloom description: insignificant flowers, usually removed
Light: ranges all the way from full shade to full sun,
     depending on variety
Water: moderate
Maintenance: low

Flanders Poppy

This hardy annual/biennial, native to Europe, has an interesting Amana connection. Although the Inspirationist religion is a pacifistic one, the story goes that a few Amana men volunteered to serve in the armed services dur-ing World War I. Finding themselves in Belgium in the fields of Flanders, they marveled at the fire-engine red poppies whose blossoms set the coun-tryside afire. They collected seed and brought it back with them on their return to Amana after the war. The gardening conditions here were ideal for growing poppies. They grew vigorously and self-sowed liberally. Even today, some gardens, including our own, sport drifts of red in spring and early summer.

Depending on when the seed germinates, the Flanders poppy is either an annual or a biennial. If the seed germinates in the fall, small plantlets will appear before the first frost. The plantlets winter over, even here where winter temperatures often dip below zero. If the seed germinates in spring, the plants will produce flowers and then die, right along with those that have wintered over and flowered at the same time.

All poppy varieties resent being transplanted, due to any disturbance of their long taproots. Flanders poppy seedlings that start in fall will have no taproot yet when they begin growing again in early spring. At that point they're transplantable. Care must be taken to dig them with enough soil, so that the roots are not exposed. Ideally, the soil should be quite moist, so that it doesn't crumble away from the roots in the transplanting process.

Hardiness (fall seedlings): zones 5 and up
Height: 12–18 inches
Spread: 10–12 inches
Bloom time: mid spring to early summer
Bloom description: bright red with a black
     polka-dot at the base of each petal
Light: full sun
Water: moderate
Maintenance: low

Flowering Spurge

(See photo 22 in color section.) This plant is native in the United States and grows in pastures, prairies, abandoned fields, stream banks, glades, open woods, inland dunes, railway beds, and roadsides. It ranges from Maine, south to Florida, west to Texas, north to South Dakota, and northeast to Minnesota. The cultivars available in the horticultural trade are every bit as beautiful as annual baby's breath and have two other advantages: they're perennial, and they have an exceedingly long bloom time. I like to weave their airy presence into the vignettes I create in our cottage garden.

Hardiness: zones 4a–6b
Height: 24–30 inches
Spread: 18–24 inches
Bloom time: late spring to late summer
Bloom description: panicles of small, white
     flowers like those of baby's breath
Light: full sun to part shade
Water: moderate
Maintenance: low

Heliopsis

(See photo 23 in color section.) Heliopsis or false sunflower is one of the stalwarts in our flower beds. It's bone hardy and has golden yellow flowers that seem to last forever. The species is native to the eastern two-thirds of North America.

'Loraine Sunshine' is a heliopsis variety I particularly treasure, because it provides additional interest to my groupings due to its unusual leaves. From the very moment that its amazing whitish foliage with prominent dark green veins emerges until the time it yields to freezing temperatures, this plant provides a welcome bit of drama. Happily, it also self-sows in our gardens, albeit very sparingly.

Hardiness: zones 3a–9b
Height: 24–36 inches
Spread: 15–18 inches
Bloom time: mid summer to frost
Bloom description: bright yellow, daisy-like
Light: full sun to mostly sun
Water: moderate
Maintenance: low

Lespedeza (Bush Clover)

(See photo 24 in color section.) I first became acquainted with lespedeza as a ninth grader, doing research for a project on soil erosion. Back then, and yet today, lespedeza was known first and foremost as an agricultural crop, raised for forage and erosion control. As a member of the legume family, it also fixes nitrogen in the soil, raising the soil's fertility. Unfortunately, some species are invasive, but several garden-worthy species are part of today's horticultural scene, although they're still lurking in the background at this point. They deserve better.

My favorite cultivar is 'Gibraltar', a pink bush clover. It has proven to be very hardy in our garden, coming back vigorously every spring. A well-behaved sub-shrub, it grows about three feet tall and about as wide. The cluster of branches arises at soil level in mid spring and grows upward and outward in graceful arches. Even when not in bloom, this plant adds beauty and interest to the garden.

When the plant is about two feet tall, growth slows until late summer, when a spurt sends the branches upward another foot or more. Soon pendant clusters of pinkish lavender flowers appear at the tips of the branches and dangle from the leaf axils along each branch. The individual blossoms, as is typical of legumes, resemble the flowers of peas. The clusters resemble miniature wisteria racemes.

To my great delight I discovered that there's an advantage to this late summer/early fall growth spurt. The shorter perennials that are neighbors to one of the lespedezas in our gardens aren't in bloom at this point in the season, and the area is devoid of color. The weeping branches hide the colorless perennials from view somewhat and fill the area with their beautiful pinkish lavender color.

Hardiness: zones 4a–9b
Height: 3–4 feet
Spread: 4–5 feet
Bloom time: late summer to mid fall
Bloom description: pinkish lavender clusters
Light: full sun to part sun
Water: moderate
Maintenance: low

Poppy Mallow

(See photo 25 in color section.) Poppy mallow is a wonderful native vine that clambers through perennials and up into shrubs, never overpowering them and providing color when other perennials have spent their blooms. It self-sows moderately in our gardens.

Hardiness: zones 5a–8b
Height: vine length varies from 24 to 48 inches
Spread: see height
Bloom time: spring to fall
Bloom description: cup-shaped magenta/fuchsia blossoms
Light: full sun to part shade
Water: moderate
Maintenance: low

Vining Asparagus Fern

(See photo 26 in color section.) Curiosity got the best of me several years ago when I read about an asparagus fern that vines up to eight feet and is truly hardy in the Midwest. It was collected in Korea's Chuwang Mountain region. The beautiful, delicate, airy vine looks stunning as it weaves its way up and over an arbor. Small white flowers grace the vine in late spring, followed by bright red berries in late summer. Its beauty increases as it produces additional shoots from one year to the next.

Hardiness: zones 5–9
Height: 8–10 feet
Spread: 2 feet
Bloom time: late spring
Bloom description: tiny, white
Light: full sun to part shade
Water: moderate
Maintenance: low

Perennial Sweet Pea

(See photo 27 in color section.) Another vine that has proven its garden worthiness is the perennial sweet pea. It weaves its way in and out between the pickets of the dark brown fence that encloses our cottage garden. The dark color of the fence offers a nice background for the white blossoms that appear in profusion from late spring to frost. The long period of bloom is a welcome characteristic in any perennial. This one also comes in pink and mauve. If it likes the growing conditions, perennial sweet pea will self-sow. Some gardeners report that it self-sows to the point of weediness, although that has never been a problem in our gardens.

Hardiness: zones 3a–9b
Height: 6 feet
Spread: 3 feet
Bloom time: late spring to frost
Bloom description: flower clusters are white,
    pink, or violet/lavender

Light: full sun to part shade
Water: moderate
Maintenance: low

Sweet Autumn Clematis

(See photo 13 in color section.) While clematis cultivars come in many beautiful colors, with both single and double flowers, one of my favorite varieties is the old stand-by sweet autumn clematis. As its name implies, sweet autumn clematis blooms in late summer or early fall and has sweet, vanilla-scented blossoms. Its huge masses of flowers often hide the leaves almost entirely. One plant climbing into our blue spruce sends up vines as high as twenty feet. While impressive during the day, it's spectacular at dusk, when its blossoms literally glow against the darker needles of the spruce.

Hardiness: zones 3a–9b
Height: up to 20 feet
Spread: up to 5 feet
Bloom time: from early fall to shortly before frost
Bloom description: small, white
Light: full sun to part shade
Water: moderate
Maintenance: low

Chinese Seven-Son Flower Tree

(See photo 19 in color section.) This tree does just about everything. It blooms in late summer, when no other trees are in flower. The double blossoms are white and are borne in clusters of seven, hence its common name. Their sweet perfume attracts bees and often great swarms of monarch butterflies. Once the petals fall off, the calyx that held them in place enlarges and turns a dusky pink. Then the tree blooms pink for several weeks. For its fall finale, if conditions are right, it produces red leaves. As if that's not enough, its bark exfoliates, revealing a light tawny orange pattern that's unique among trees of any variety. What's more, it's extremely hardy, has no serious insect or disease problems, and is adaptable to most any soil type. It grows to about twenty feet at maturity, with a loose, open habit. The best flower display occurs when it's planted in full sun.

The Chinese seven-son flower tree has an interesting history. Plant explorer Ernest H. Wilson (1876–1930) introduced it to the Western Hemisphere. Wilson was employed by Harvard University's Arnold Arboretum to travel the world seeking rare plants. He found the seven-son flower tree in the Zhejiang Province in China. It flourished at the arboretum but remained obscure. Eventually it died without anyone showing any particular interest in it. In fact, in 1980 it had to be reintroduced from China, where, ironically, it's now rare.

Given its many good qualities, it seems incredible that no one in the United States was growing this plant. Stephen Spongberg, horticultural taxonomist at the Arnold Arboretum and a member of the 1980 expedition, brought a specimen back with him. He recently noted, via the University of British Columbia Botanical Garden's website, that "today there are undoubtedly more individual plants in cultivation in North America than in all of China." Through the arboretum's promotional efforts, the nursery trade finally sat up and took notice of this remarkable plant. In a relatively short period, the nursery community has embraced this outstanding tree and has begun to make it available to the public once more.

Hardiness: zones 5a–9b
   (although some sources include zone 4)
Height: 20 feet
Spread: up to 10 feet
Bloom time: summer
Bloom description: white, double, fragrant,
   borne in clusters of seven
Light: full sun
Water: moderate
Maintenance: low

Persicaria

Persicarias, known collectively as smartweeds, fleeceflowers, or knotweeds, number over fifty species, some of which are definitely not garden-worthy. They range in height from six inches or less to an imposing six feet. The three we grow in our gardens are giant fleeceflower, 'Painter's Palette', and 'Firetail'. We have two clumps of fleeceflower at the rear of our white garden.

When it's six feet tall and wide, most garden visitors assume that it's a shrub. They're amazed, as I was, that something that large and that exuberant starts out at ground level each spring. Although some persicarias self-sow to the point of weediness, the giant fleeceflowers gracing our gardens for the past six years have produced nary a seed.

Unfortunately, that's not true of 'Painter's Palette'. The trade-off, though, is worth it. I love the berry-juice-colored squiggles across its white and green leaves. It has filled an entire bed along our driveway, which is also the main entrance to our gardens. Visitors never fail to comment on its unique beauty. I also value its delicate sprays of tiny scarlet blossoms in late summer. They make interesting fillers in flower arrangements. Think of them as red baby's breath. Almost as important to me as the unusual leaves is the fact that they emerge later in the spring than those of most other perennials. I've taken advantage of this habit by under-planting the entire bed with early tulips, Roman hyacinths, and daffodils. The foliage of these spring bulbs is already starting to die off when the slender shoots of 'Painter's Palette' make their appearance. As this persicaria grows rapidly to a mature height of about 20 inches, it soon hides the unsightly bulb foliage completely.

I use 'Firetail' to hide unsightly growth, or rather lack thereof, as well. The subjects to be hidden here are the "legs" of roses, especially those of climbers, that have lost their leaves from the ground up to about two feet by mid summer. The bare, very thorny canes of these roses are not only unsightly but downright menacing, especially if I'm weeding or mulching in their vicinity. Their exuberant growth and reddish, tail-like blooms cover the bare canes beautifully. Unlike the meandering 'Painter's Palette', 'Firetail' stays put in an ever-expanding clump. Simply divide it when it gets too big and share some with fellow gardeners or find another spot for it in your own garden.

GIANT FLEECEFLOWER
Hardiness: zones 4a–9b
Height: 6 feet
Spread: 6 feet
Bloom time: late spring to fall
Bloom description: dense, frothy panicles
of small ivory blossoms

Light: full sun to part shade
Water: moderate
Maintenance: low

'PAINTER'S PALETTE' (See photo 28 in color section.)
Hardiness: zones 4a–10b
Height: 18–24 inches
Spread: 18 inches
Bloom time: mid summer
Bloom description: loose panicles of tiny scarlet blossoms
Light: sun to partial shade (a bit of shade produces
    brighter leaf coloration)
Water: moderate
Maintenance: low

'FIRETAIL'
Hardiness: zones 4a–7b
Height: 3 feet
Spread: 3 feet
Bloom time: spring to frost
Bloom description: slender, red, bottle-brush-shaped
    flower tails
Light: full sun to part shade
Water: moderate
Maintenance: low

Petunia

(See photo 29 in color section.) There's no doubt that petunias are one of the most popular bedding plants ever grown. The array of colors, shapes, sizes, and habits is phenomenal.

It wasn't always like this, though. I can remember the pastel shades of pink, lavender, and purple on somewhat sprawling plants that graced my mother's flower beds. Occasionally a white one or even one with the coveted star pattern would pop up. And pop up they did, self-sowing liberally, not only in the beds but even in cracks in the sidewalk.

That's basically all there was. No supertunias, no wave petunias, no grandifloras, hedgifloras, multifloras, millifloras, or floribundas. No yellows, reds, blues, pinks edged in green, picotees, ruffled blossoms, or doubles.

Philibert Commerson, a circumnavigator and naturalist, provided the first inkling of the petunia's existence while in Argentina in the early 1790s. It wasn't until the 1820s that the two parents of the modern petunia first appeared together in Europe, thanks to Scotsman John Tweedie.

In 1825, at the age of 50, Tweedie left his job as a landscape gardener at Eglinton Castle and at the Royal Botanical Garden in Edinburgh. He packed up his wife and six children and set sail for Argentina. He soon proved to be a plant explorer of some repute and promptly sent back home two wild petunias, the white *Petunia nyctaginiflora* (also known as *Petunia axillaris*) and the light purple *Petunia violacea*. These two species are the parent stock of all modern petunias. They caused quite a stir all across Europe and ignited frenzied cross-breeding programs. Those programs yielded new colors, larger flowers, sweetly scented flowers, and even double flowers.

One of my favorite petunias at the moment is supertunia 'Raspberry Blast'. It's a stunning plant that has earned many top awards. Its pink blooms are edged in deep cerise violet, a real wow factor. It has a trailing habit and is a very low-maintenance petunia.

Hardiness: zones 10a–11b; treat as an annual in all other zones
Height: 6–8 inches
Spread: 4 feet (trailing)
Bloom time: all season
Bloom description: pink, edged in deep cerise violet
Light: full sun
Water: moderate
Maintenance: low

Geranium 'Rozanne'

(See photo 30 in color section.) Of all the popular perennial geraniums available today, 'Rozanne' is the one that has performed best in our gardens. It has exceptional heat tolerance and, once started, it flowers nonstop. The large, five-petaled, violet-blue flowers have purple veins and white centers. Foliage is deeply cut, slightly marbled, and deep green.

Hardiness: zones 5a–8b
Height: 12–18 inches
Spread: 1–2 feet
Bloom time: May to frost
Bloom description: violet blue with white centers
Light: full sun to part shade
Water: moderate
Maintenance: low

Rudbeckia 'Henry Eilers'

(See photo 31 in color section.) This plant is a hardy native of the Midwest that Henry Eilers collected from a prairie remnant along a railroad bed in southern Illinois. It was introduced into the horticultural trade in 2003. Flower stalks begin to form in mid spring, sometimes reaching five feet by flowering time in August. The flowers are unusual in that the yellow ray petals are rolled instead of flat, giving the flowers a quilled effect. They bloom in clusters atop strong, sometimes-branching stems from July to September. This rudbeckia always draws comments from our visitors.

Hardiness: zones 4a–8b
Height: 3–5 feet
Spread: 1–2 feet
Bloom time: July to September
Bloom description: yellow rolled ray petals
    with a brown center disk
Light: full sun
Water: moderate
Maintenance: low

Tree Peony

(See photo 32 in color section.) The major difference between herbaceous peonies and tree peonies is that the woody stems of tree peonies don't die to the ground in the winter. Except for dead wood, don't prune tree peonies unless you don't mind eliminating some buds for next year's blossoms. Like herbaceous peonies, tree peonies are tough, long-lived plants. Their large blossoms are among the most spectacular in any temperate zone garden. Unfortunately, they only last for about a week.

Among the tree peonies we grow, the cultivar 'Shimanishiki' has the most stunning blossoms. The double blooms have snow white petals with irregular narrow and wide vertical streaks of crimson. This is another literal traffic stopper in our gardens.

Hardiness: zones 4a–8b
Height: 3–5 feet
Spread: 3–4 feet
Bloom time: early spring
Bloom description: large, very showy; many colors, including red,
     white, pink, coral, lavender, cream, yellow, purple, magenta,
     and numerous bicolors
Light: full sun to part shade
Water: moderate
Maintenance: low

Tulip 'Rob Vanderlinden'

(See photo 33 in color section.) 'Rob Vanderlinden' is known not only for its large, brilliant scarlet flowers but for its outstanding decorative foliage, which is mottled and edged in white. This unique foliage adds some interest to our tulip beds even before the flowers appear. It's a hybridized *greigii* species tulip, which means that if it likes its growing conditions, it'll perennialize and multiply. No need to order new bulbs every year. Somewhat difficult to find, this tulip deserves to be much more widely known than it is currently. *Greigii* tulips are native to Turkestan.

Hardiness: zones 3a–7b
Height: 10–12 inches
Spread: leaf spread is about 8 inches
Bloom time: early spring
Bloom description: large, bright scarlet, cup-shaped blossoms
Light: full sun to part shade
Water: moderate
Maintenance: low

'John Cabot' Rose

(See photo 34 in color section.) The Prestele-inspired trellis on the south wall of our house's exterior is home to a rose called 'John Cabot', a super-hardy, disease-resistant, semi-climbing, fuchsia-red rose. One of the Canadian explorer series roses developed at the Morden Research Station in Manitoba, it survives relatively severe winters down to −30 degrees Fahrenheit.

'John Cabot' replaces an unknown variety that required me to tie the canes up in the spring, untie them in the fall, lay them down against the foundation, and cover them with leaves and old rag carpets if I wanted the canes to survive. With this Canadian rose, I can simply leave the canes tied to the trellis and have absolutely no winter dieback. What's more, after its first flush of blossoms in spring, it continues to bloom throughout the whole season. What a time-and-effort saver!

Hardiness: zones 3a–9b
Height: 6–8 feet
Spread: 6–8 feet
Bloom time: all season
Bloom description: double, cupped, pinkish red
Light: full sun to part shade
Water: moderate
Maintenance: low

Yellow Corydalis

(See photo 35 in color section.) This corydalis species has been a happy surprise in our gardens. After reading cautionary statements about its need for light shade and good moisture, its general intolerance of hot and humid summer conditions, its short-lived perennial nature, and its aggressive self-sowing under optimum conditions, I didn't have much hope for its success in our gardens. Adding to that my general gardening philosophy of not tolerating plants that don't perform well on their own, it would appear that yellow corydalis had little chance of success at Cottage-in-the-Meadow Gardens.

Even so, I decided to give it that chance, because the yellow color of its blossoms was a good fit with my color scheme. I loved its delicate foliage, and I did have a spot for it in light shade with good moisture. Within three years, from the one specimen I planted, I had a patch of corydalis about six feet square. Not only that, but the plants kept on producing flowers right through the heat and humidity of our summer. When a few plants volunteered in a nearby planting of hostas, I loved the combination. But I got the biggest surprise of all when a volunteer popped up in a patch of ground that was dry and received at least half a day of direct sun. It not only survived, it actually thrived. Its leaves were a bit sun-bleached, sort of a gray-green color, but not at all unattractive. While plantlets keep showing up in new places in our beds, the reseeding hasn't in any way been aggressive.

Hardiness: zones 4a–8b
Height: 8–12 inches
Spread: 9–12 inches
Bloom time: spring through fall
Bloom description: yellow blossoms borne in
    racemes on short, branched, leafy stems
Light: full shade to part sun
Water: moderate
Maintenance: low

Grant Wood Sansevieria

(See photo 36 in color section.) For his painting *Woman with Plants*, Iowa artist Grant Wood used one of his mother's mother-in-law's tongue plants as a model. Several years ago I had the good fortune of getting a descendant of that plant from a friend. The original divisions from the plant were given to friends by Esther Armstrong, the wife of a department store executive in downtown Cedar Rapids, Iowa, who got her plant from the Wood family. She died in 2002 at age 99. The lineage, starting with Hattie Wood, Grant Wood's mother, is as follows: Esther Armstrong, Joan Liffring-Zug Bourret (Iowa photographer, author, and publisher), Peter Hoehnle (Amana historian), Larry Rettig. There's even a Hattie Wood Sansevieria Club, composed of folks who have descendants of her plant.

Hardiness: zones 10–11
Height: 18–24 inches
Spread: 6–12 inches

Bloom time: summer
Bloom description: cream blossoms borne
    in racemes on branched stems
Light: full shade to part sun
Water: moderate, drought tolerant
Maintenance: low

Connie Zuber Canna

(See photo 37 in color section.) This canna is associated with Bill Zuber, who grew up in my native village of Middle Amana. He played on local baseball teams after Amana's reorganization in 1932 and proved to be a pitcher of considerable talent. Working his way up through various ball teams, Bill began an eleven-year Major League career in 1936. He pitched with the Cleveland Indians, Washington Senators, New York Yankees, and Boston Red Sox.

After pitching twenty games for the Red Sox during the 1947 season, Bill retired to the Amana village of Homestead, Iowa. There with his wife Connie, he launched a very popular restaurant, Bill Zuber's Dugout, in 1949. As a celebratory gift during the restaurant's grand opening, Bill's mother gave Connie a division of one of her prized cannas. Connie, in turn, gave me the plant for safe keeping several years ago. I intend to pass it on to next-generation gardeners. Bill passed away in 1982, but Connie, now in her nineties, still keeps an active interest in gardening.

CREATIVITY IN AND OUT
OF THE GARDENS

I LOVE THE BEAUTY that the world of plants offers us, so I don't really mind the weeding, mulching, watering, and feeding they require to look their best. But I like to interact with our gardens in more creative ways, aside from plant placement and color schemes. In this chapter and the next, I'll share with you ways in which Wilma and I do just that.

We'll take a look at garden produce first. Cooking and food presentation are arts that allow us to be creative with the food we raise. Next is a section on hammered botanical prints, where I describe how to produce artistic plant images by taking fresh garden material and hammering it into watercolor paper. Additional directions are included for a special centerpiece, several wreaths, a gnome home, and a garden fountain incorporating rocks where water would be expected.

Garden produce has a beauty all its own. The reds, pinks, and yellows of tomatoes and some peppers punctuate the more predominant greens. Beans and summer squash add larger splashes of yellow. The dark beauty of ripening eggplants provides late-summer interest. Then there's a veritable symphony of vegetable and leaf sizes, shapes, and textures.

Creativity enters the picture not only with a pleasing garden layout, but with what one does with the produce once it's harvested. Food presentation at the table allows for all kinds of imaginative approaches, from watermelon baskets to a seemingly endless variety of garnishes.

Recipes

Creating or modifying recipes is obviously a way to express oneself, using food as a medium. Here's a sampling of Wilma's recipes containing produce raised in our gardens. I'll let her do the talking in this section.

Salads

WILMA'S COLESLAW

1 cup shredded cabbage	3 teaspoons sugar
1 diced apple	2 tablespoons orange juice
2 tablespoons mayonnaise	Raisins to taste

Combine dressing ingredients. Add cabbage, raisins, and apple, mixing thoroughly.

POPPY SEED DRESSING FOR SPINACH SALAD

1 cup salad oil	1 tablespoon grated onion
½ cup sugar	1 teaspoon salt
⅓ cup cider vinegar	1 teaspoon dry mustard
1 tablespoon poppy seeds	Spinach

In blender at medium speed, blend all dressing ingredients (save the spinach) until mixed. Dressing will be thick. Drizzle on spinach as desired. Store in tightly covered jar in refrigerator. Stir well before using. Makes about one and one-half cups.

RETTICH SALAAT

(Radish Salad, original Amana Radish available from our seed bank)

2 cups grated radishes	¼ teaspoon salt
1 tablespoon vinegar	dash of pepper
1 tablespoon minced chives	2 tablespoons sour cream

Add salt to grated radishes and let stand one hour. Drain and add the remaining ingredients.

EIER SALAAT

(Egg Lettuce Salad, original Amana lettuce available from our seed bank)

Roughly equal parts of:

Chopped green onion	Chopped, hard cooked egg
Chopped radishes	Lettuce

Harvest lettuce by cutting the tops off the lettuce plants. Do not pull the lettuce, as it will continue to grow. Wash, shake off excess water, and wrap in a towel. Store in the refrigerator to crisp. When ready to serve, add chopped green onion, chopped radishes, and the following dressing. Top with chopped, hard cooked egg.

DRESSING

1 cup mayonnaise	4 tablespoons milk
¼ teaspoon salt	4 tablespoons sweet pickle juice
¼ teaspoon Accent seasoning (optional)	¼ teaspoon Italian seasoning
	2 tablespoons sugar
Dash of pepper	

Thoroughly combine all dressing ingredients. This makes about one and one-half cups dressing.

WILMA'S PICKLED RED CABBAGE

4 cups shredded red cabbage	¾ cup sugar
¾ cup vinegar	½ teaspoon salt
1 cup water	

Sprinkle shredded cabbage with salt and place in bowl. Combine remaining ingredients and bring to a boil. Pour over cabbage while hot. Refrigerate twenty-four hours before serving.

CARROT SALAD

3 medium carrots, grated	¼ cup raisins
¼ cup chopped celery	Chopped bell pepper (optional)
1 apple, cored and diced	Mayonnaise to moisten

Combine all ingredients and chill.

Soups

WILMA'S DUMPLING SOUP

4 cups chicken broth	2 tablespoons butter or margarine
2 tablespoons chopped onion	½ cup water (boiling)
2 tablespoons chopped parsley	¼ cup flour
1 egg	

Add onion and parsley to chicken broth and simmer five minutes. Meanwhile, melt butter in boiling water. Quickly add flour and stir constantly until dough "follows" spoon. Remove from heat and stir in egg. Beat until dough is smooth. Return to heat and stir one minute. Drop by spoonfuls into simmering broth. Simmer five more minutes. Season to taste.

MOM'S TOMATO SOUP

1 quart tomatoes, peeled and cut into chunks	1 large sprig parsley
½ green bell pepper, chopped	2 tablespoons sugar
1 stalk celery, chopped	½ tablespoon flour, dissolved in tomato juice
2 small onions, chopped	

Combine first five ingredients and simmer, stirring occasionally, until all vegetables are soft. Transfer to ricer and rice. Pour riced vegetables and tomato juice into saucepan. Add flour–tomato juice mixture. Add sugar and salt to taste. Heat, stirring occasionally.

BORSHT
(Beet Soup)

4 to 5 beets, fist-size	1 teaspoon marjoram
1 large onion	1 teaspoon thyme
1 large garlic clove	2 teaspoons dill
2 cups beef stock	Sour cream
Dash of salt	1 tablespoon butter
Dash of black pepper	

Boil and peel beets and chop into cubes. Sauté onion in butter, then add garlic and brown. Stir in beets. Add stock and herbs. Simmer twenty minutes. Purée. Serve with a dollop of sour cream and, if desired, a sprinkle of dill. May be served hot or cold.

WILMA'S POTATO SOUP

2 quarts water	1 large celery stalk, chopped
4 beef boullion cubes	1 large onion, chopped
1 large garlic clove, chopped	4 cups grated potatoes

Bring water to boil. Add rest of ingredients. Simmer thirty minutes. Strain and reserve liquid. Place remaining ingredients in food processor and process until smooth. Add to reserved liquid. Season to taste. Optional toppings: chopped green onion, chopped chives, parsley, paprika, bacon bits. (Use your imagination!)

ASPARAGUS SOUP

¼ cup butter	2 medium potatoes
1 medium onion	2 tablespoons fresh basil leaves
1 stalk celery, with leaves	2 cups heavy cream
4 cups chicken broth or vegetable stock	Salt and pepper to taste
3 pounds fresh (or frozen) asparagus	

Chop onion and celery. Break off woody ends of asparagus and discard. Cut stalks into one-inch pieces. Peel and dice potatoes. Mince basil leaves. Melt butter in soup kettle. Sauté onion and celery until softened, about two to three minutes. Add stock, asparagus pieces, potatoes, and basil. Cover pot and cook twenty minutes or until vegetables are tender. Stir occasionally. Purée in small batches in blender. Add purée to kettle and blend in cream. Season with salt and pepper. Warm soup carefully, do not boil.

PEA SOUP

2 cups large peas (Overly ripe peas from the garden work well.)	2 tablespoons cornstarch
	Bacon bits
	Salt
1½ cups meat broth	Seasoned pepper
1½ cups milk	

Cook peas in meat broth for thirty minutes. Drain, reserving broth. Put peas through ricer and add to broth. Blend cornstarch and milk in a cup. Stir into soup. Season with bacon bits, salt, and seasoned pepper. Cook and stir until soup reaches desired thickness.

Sweet Breads and Rolls

CHOCOLATE ZUCCHINI BREAD

3 cups flour	1 cup oil
3 cups sugar	3 cups grated zucchini
1 teaspoon baking soda	2 teaspoons vanilla
½ cup cocoa	1 cup chopped nuts
Dash of salt	4 eggs
1½ teaspoons baking powder	

Cut wax paper to fit in the bottoms of two 9 × 5-inch loaf pans. Grease wax paper. Combine dry ingredients. Mix in oil, eggs, and vanilla. Add zucchini and nuts. Pour into pans and bake at 350 degrees for about seventy-five minutes.

CARROT BREAD

1½ cups flour	1 teaspoon cinnamon
½ teaspoon baking soda	½ cup oil
Dash of salt	1 egg
¼ teaspoon baking powder	1 cup shredded carrots
½ cup sugar	½ chopped nuts
½ cup brown sugar	½ cup raisins

Cut wax paper to fit in the bottom of an 8 × 4 × 2-inch loaf pan. Grease wax paper. Combine dry ingredients except brown sugar, then stir in brown sugar, oil, egg, and carrots. Fold in nuts and raisins. Pour into prepared pan. Bake at 350 degrees for one hour or until toothpick comes out clean. Cool ten minutes and remove from pan.

APPLE BREAD

1 cup sugar	2 cups chopped apples
½ cup shortening	1½ tablespoons milk
2 cups flour	½ teaspoon vanilla
1 teaspoon baking soda	1 cup chopped nuts
¼ teaspoon salt	Cinnamon sugar
2 eggs	

Cut wax paper to fit in the bottom of an 8 × 4 × 2-inch loaf pan. Grease
wax paper. Cream shortening and sugar. Mix in eggs, vanilla, and milk.
Combine and add dry ingredients. Fold in apples and nuts. Pour into loaf
pan and top with cinnamon sugar. Bake at 350 degrees for one hour.

POTATO ROLLS

3 to 4 cups flour	1¼ cups water
½ cup mashed potatoes	(tap or reserved from
3 tablespoons sugar	cooking potatoes)
2 packages quick-rise yeast	3 tablespoons butter
1 teaspoon salt	

Combine two cups flour, mashed potatoes, sugar, yeast, and salt in large
bowl. Heat water and butter to 130 degrees. Stir into yeast mix. Add enough
flour to make soft dough. Knead until smooth and elastic. Cover and let
rest ten minutes. Divide dough into sixteen pieces and shape into balls.
Place into two greased 9-inch cake pans. Cover and let rise until doubled.
Bake at 400 degrees for about twenty minutes. Can also be shaped into a
bread loaf.

POPPY SEED DINNER ROLLS

1 package quick-rise yeast	2 tablespoons honey
½ teaspoon salt	1½ cups milk
5 to 6 cups flour	2 large eggs
4 tablespoons margarine or butter	½ cup poppy seeds

Combine yeast, salt, and two cups flour. In small saucepan, combine butter,
honey, and milk, and heat to 125 degrees. Add liquid to dry ingredients and
beat two minutes at medium speed. Beat in one egg, one egg white, and one
cup flour. Beat another two minutes. Using wooden spoon, stir in poppy
seeds. Add remaining flour to make stiff dough. Knead until smooth.
Place dough in greased bowl, turning to grease top. Cover and let rise until
doubled. Punch down and let rest ten minutes. Shape into knots, clover
leaves, or balls and place on cookie sheet about two inches apart. Let rise
fifteen minutes. Combine egg yolk and two teaspoons milk. Brush on rolls.
Bake at 375 degrees for about fifteen minutes, until golden.

GROUND CHERRY JAM FOR ROLLS
(*Kapsul Schmiersel*)

Schmiersel is the South Amana dialect word for "jam." Most of the German-speaking residents of the other Amana villages say *Schillee*. This recipe came from my mother, who used to make it for sale. I still make it this way, but my sister uses Sure-Jell.

4 cups hulled, washed ground cherries
½ small lemon, chopped, seeds removed
3 cups sugar
¼ cup water

Combine all ingredients and simmer. Jam is done when a small amount is dropped on a plate, and you can draw a path through it with your finger. This can take anywhere from twenty to forty-five minutes. Put in jars and freeze until ready to use.

Vegetables

EUROPEAN BLACK SALSIFY
(*Schwartswortsel*, available from our seed bank)

2 cups scraped root cut into 1-inch lengths
Enough broth to cover the chopped roots
　　(from boiled pork sausage or chicken)
2 tablespoons melted butter or margarine
2 tablespoons flour

Scrape the roots until the outside black layer is gone. Immediately soak in milk or water. When all the roots are scraped, cut into one-inch pieces. Boil in meat broth until tender. Drain, and save the broth.

Melt butter or margarine. Stir in two tablespoons flour. Slowly stir in one cup of reserved broth. Cook over low heat until thickened. Add the cooked salsify and heat through. If you have a large quantity, the salsify can be put in jars and frozen until ready to eat.

AMANA SPINACH

1 cup frozen, chopped spinach
1 tablespoon chopped onion
2 tablespoons margarine
2 tablespoons dry bread crumbs

2 tablespoons flour
Salt and pepper to taste
1 cup beef stock

Melt margarine, and brown the onions and bread crumbs. Stir in flour. Slowly add beef stock, and cook until thickened. Season to taste. Add thawed spinach. Heat through.

MOM'S *KARDOFFELKLEES*
(Potato Dumplings)

4 cups cold, ground-up
   cooked potatoes
1½–2 cups buttered bread cubes
1 large or 2 small eggs
1 large chopped onion

4 tablespoons flour
1 teaspoon salt
½ teaspoon ground marjoram
6 inches of celery, chopped

Combine all ingredients. Using hands (floured, if necessary), form into twelve balls. If sticky, roll in flour (can be frozen at this point). To cook, steam in small amount of boiling water. Can also be heated in microwave. Top with buttered, browned bread crumbs.

WILMA'S BACON LIMA BEANS

4 slices diced bacon
2 sliced celery stalks
Dash of salt

Dash of black pepper
2 to 3 tablespoons water
10 ounces of lima beans

Cook bacon until browned. Drain bacon, saving two tablespoons drippings. Sauté celery, beans, and seasonings five to ten minutes until beans are almost tender. Add water and simmer five minutes until tender. Sprinkle with bacon.

PHILLY POTATOES

4 cups hot mashed potatoes	¼ cup chopped pimento
1 egg	1 teaspoon salt
8 ounces cream cheese	Dash of black pepper
⅓ cup chopped onion	

Combine hot potatoes, egg, cream cheese, and seasonings in mixer bowl and mix thoroughly. Carefully stir in onion and pimento. Transfer to 10-inch greased casserole bowl. Bake at 350 degrees for forty-five minutes or until completely heated through.

VEGGIE PIZZA

1 package crescent rolls	1 to 2 cups shredded cheddar cheese
4 ounces cream cheese	Favorite vegetables (such as peas, chopped
¼ cup mayonnaise	celery, and shredded carrots)
1 teaspoon dry ranch dressing mix	Meat: bacon, chopped pepperoni, cooked ham, or chicken

Press crescent rolls together and roll into a big square. Bake at 375 degrees for twelve minutes. Cool. Combine cream cheese, mayonnaise, and ranch dressing and spread over crust. Top with your favorite vegetables and meat(s), and sprinkle with shredded cheddar cheese.

Meats

CHICKEN WITH BASIL AND CREAM SAUCE

2 whole large skinless boneless
  chicken breasts
¼ cup milk
¼ cup seasoned dried bread crumbs
3 tablespoons butter or margarine
½ teaspoon chicken flavored
  instant bouillon
1 cup heavy cream

4 ounces pimentos,
  sliced ¼ inch thick
½ cup packed thinly sliced
  fresh basil leaves
¼ cup grated Parmesan cheese
⅛ teaspoon pepper
Fresh basil sprigs for garnish

Cut each chicken breast in half. Pour milk into pie plate. Place bread
crumbs on wax paper. Dip chicken breasts into milk, then into bread
crumbs to coat. In 12-inch skillet over medium-high heat, melt butter or
margarine and add chicken breasts. Cook until fork-tender and golden
brown on both sides, about ten minutes. Arrange chicken on warm
platter and keep warm. Stir bouillon and water into the same skillet. Over
medium-high heat, heat to boiling, stirring to loosen brown bits. Stir in
heavy cream and sliced pimentos. With heat on high, heat to boiling. Cook
for one minute, stirring frequently. Reduce heat to medium, add sliced
basil, grated Parmesan, and pepper. Pour sauce over chicken breasts.
Garnish with fresh basil sprigs.

ELEVEN MINUTE MEAT LOAF

1 pound lean ground beef
1 beaten egg
6 crushed soda crackers
1 small chopped onion
1 tablespoon chopped parsley

¾ teaspoon salt
¼ teaspoon seasoned pepper
¼ cup chopped green pepper
¼ cup chopped celery
½ cup ketchup

Mix all ingredients and spoon into uncovered, greased casserole dish.
Cook in microwave for eleven minutes.

AMANA-STYLE SWISS STEAK

1½ pounds round steak   ¾ cup salt
1½ tablespoons shortening   1 medium chopped onion
¼ cup flour   ½ cup vinegar

Combine flour, salt, and a dash of pepper and pound into steak. Lightly brown both sides of steak in shortening. Add vinegar and simmer just until the liquid evaporates. Add chopped onion and cover steak with water. Cover and bake at 300 degrees for two hours or until tender.

PORK LOIN ROAST WITH APPLE CREAM

4-pound boneless pork loin roast   2 tablespoons brown sugar
1 cup applesauce   1 cup apple juice
1 garlic clove, slivered   ½ cup whipping cream
1 large tart apple
2 tablespoons melted butter
   or margarine

Cut small slits in roast and insert slivered garlic. Rub meat with salt and pepper. Roast at 450 degrees for thirty minutes. Reduce oven temperature to 350 degrees and add butter and apple juice to roast. Continue baking sixty minutes, basting occasionally. Remove roast from oven and remove all but one-quarter cup of pan juices. Slice apple thinly and place in bottom of pan. Sprinkle with brown sugar. Place roast on top, and top the roast with applesauce. Bake another ten minutes or until roast tests done. Scrape applesauce off roast into pan, and remove roast to slice. Add cream to pan contents. Bake five minutes until gravy is warm. Serve with roast.

AMANA PICKLED HAM

4 cups cubed ham
1 large sliced onion
2 cups water
1 cup vinegar

Combine all ingredients and let stand at room temperature for four hours, then refrigerate.

Desserts

GROUND CHERRY KUCHEN
(*Kapsul Kuche,* seeds available from our seed bank)

Crust:

2 cups white flour

½ cup sugar

¾ cup milk

2 teaspoons baking powder

¼ cup shortening

1 package yeast (optional)
(This dough does not rise—I add yeast
because we like the yeast flavor.)
Approximately 2 cups of ground cherries

Combine all the crust ingredients and mix well. Using floured hands, press the dough into two greased 9-inch pie pans. Arrange fruit on top. You can use any kind of fruit you like for this recipe. Pour custard topping over the fruit.

Custard Topping:

1 cup milk

2 tablespoons flour

1 cup sugar

2 eggs

Bake at 425 degrees for ten minutes. Reduce heat to 325 degrees and continue baking until the fruit is soft and custard is set. Total baking time may vary anywhere from forty-five to sixty minutes, depending on the fruit you use.

GLADY'S COFFEE CAKE

1 stick butter

1 cup sugar

1 cup flour

1 teaspoon baking powder

1 teaspoon vanilla

2 eggs

Fresh fruit

Cinnamon sugar

Cream butter and sugar. Mix in eggs, then flour and baking powder. Add vanilla. Pour into 9-inch greased cake pan. Arrange fruit on top and sprinkle with cinnamon sugar. Bake forty-five minutes at 350 degrees.

ELEGANT STRAWBERRY PIE

4 cups whole strawberries	3 tablespoons cornstarch
1 cup sugar	¼ cup strawberry gelatin
1 cup water	1 pie crust, baked

Mix cornstarch, sugar, and water. Heat until thickened, stirring constantly. Add gelatin. Cool until lukewarm. Gently stir in berries and chill until set.

STRAWBERRY RHUBARB PIE

1½ cups sugar	3 cups chopped rhubarb
½ cup flour	1 cup sliced strawberries
Dash of salt	1 tablespoon butter
¼ teaspoon cinnamon	1 pastry shell

Mix sugar, flour, salt, and cinnamon. Add fruit. Let stand twenty minutes. Spoon into pastry shell. Dot with butter. Bake at 400 degrees for forty to forty-five minutes. Lattice crust on top is optional.

APPLE TART

2 cups flour	1 teaspoon vanilla
⅓ cup sugar	4 cups peeled, sliced apples
2 teaspoons baking powder	⅔ cup apricot or peach jam,
⅔ cup butter	mixed with ¼ cup sugar
1 egg	Extra milk and sugar
¼ cup milk	

Combine flour, sugar, and baking powder and cut in butter until crumbly. In another bowl, mix egg with milk and vanilla. Add to flour mixture and mix well. Knead gently on lightly floured surface until smooth. Cover and chill one-third of dough. Pat remainder on bottom and up sides of a 9- or 10-inch tart pan with removable bottom. Arrange apples over pastry. Top with jam/sugar mixture. Roll remaining dough into ten-inch circle and cut into strips. Arrange lattice-style over apples and tuck in edges. Brush with milk and sprinkle with sugar. Bake at 375 degrees for forty-five to fifty minutes.

CHEDDAR PEAR CRISP

2½ pounds fresh pears   1 tablespoon cornstarch
1 tablespoon lemon juice   ¼ teaspoon cinnamon
½ cup sugar

Topping:
⅔ cup shredded cheddar cheese
¼ cup sugar
⅔ cup flour
3 tablespoons melted butter

Pare, core, and slice pears. Place in bowl and sprinkle with lemon juice. Mix sugar, cornstarch, and cinnamon and sprinkle over pears. Toss to coat. Place in 9-inch pie plate. Prepare topping by combining all ingredients until crumbly. Sprinkle over pear mixture. Bake at 425 degrees for twenty-five to thirty minutes.

Hammered Botanical Prints

A number of Christmases ago, I expressed an interest in flower pounding, a decorative craft that has been around for decades. Wilma picked up on my not-so-subtle hint and presented me with a how-to book. In a nutshell, the process involves taking live plant material, taping it down on a piece of fabric, and then pounding it into the material with a hammer to produce an image.

After doing a few poundings on muslin and other kinds of fabric the next spring, I felt frustration set in. It wasn't so much because of the degree of difficulty (which can be considerable), but because I felt the images were beautiful and substantial enough to stand on their own as works of art. Fabric just didn't seem to be the best medium.

In my quest to elevate flower pounding to an art form, I hit upon the idea of using watercolor paper instead of fabric. This would take the images out of the realm of decoration, allowing the viewer's focus to fall solely on the images themselves. I soon discovered that not just any watercolor paper would do. My search ended happily when I discovered Arches of France, a company with five hundred years of experience in producing paper. There are a number of types, sizes, and weights of paper to choose from. I generally use cold press, 30" × 31" sheets of 140-pound paper and cut them to size. They're somewhat pricey, but certainly not a budget buster.

The process begins with the selection of live plant material from the gardens, such as blossom petals, leaves, and stems. Before they are incorporated into a print, I create a proof of each piece of material to determine its water content. If it contains too much moisture, the result is generally a nondescript, unusable blob of color on the paper. If it contains too little moisture, little or no color transfers from the material to the paper.

Both proofing and actually creating a finished work involve the same process. I position the plant material on the watercolor paper and then tape it down with masking tape. When it comes to tape quality, cheaper is generally better. Inexpensive tape is thinner and somewhat transparent, allowing me to monitor what's going on under the tape as I hammer. It also is less sticky, decreasing the danger of taking some of the paper along with it when I remove the tape.

Using a small tack hammer with a flat, square head, I begin hammering the tape-covered material to release its color and create an image on the paper. Proofing helps me determine how hard I need to hammer to produce the desired image. A very hard hammering surface produces the best image in most instances. I use Formica mounted on a hardwood base.

When I'm done hammering, I slowly remove the tape and, with it, the remaining plant material, being careful not to smear the image or create blotches from dripping or falling debris. As a rule, I don't take the tape off all the way at first. If I spot an area that needs more hammering as I pull up the tape, I simply put the tape back down and hammer that area some more.

After allowing the paper to dry for a few minutes, I hammer more material into it until the desired image is complete. When the paper is dry, I spray it with an acrylic fixative to protect the print and to make sure that any desired plant residue will adhere to the paper permanently.

I find this kind of artistic expression very satisfying. There's something magical about being able to create beauty not only by planting and maintaining our gardens but also by using living material from them to create art in a new and exciting way. (See photo 38 in color section.)

A Della Robbia Centerpiece
for Your Holiday Table

Della Robbia refers to an artistic style that was characteristic of art produced by the fifteenth-century Italian sculptor Luca della Robbia (1400–1482) and other members of his family. As a decorative element in borders, their artwork incorporated various fruits, usually oranges, apples, pears, and grapes. This fruit motif eventually found its way into live arrangements, primarily garlands and wreaths. Such creations became known simply as della Robbia. (See photo 39 in color section.)

In the United States, della Robbia found expression in the Colonial Revival movement of the early twentieth century. An article in a 1926 issue of *House Beautiful*, for example, states: "Of late years, besides the staple wreaths of plain greens to which we have long been accustomed, the holiday's emblems have blossomed forth—or perhaps we should say fruited forth—with richness of color produced by the use of either natural or artificial fruit as an embellishment. Gorgeous Italian carvings and terra cottas of the Renaissance undoubtedly contributed to this idea."

Williamsburg, Virginia, offers perhaps the most familiar expression of della Robbia during the holiday season. In the late 1930s, Louise Fisher was in charge of flowers and Christmas decorations in Williamsburg and hit upon the idea of incorporating fresh fruit into the ordinary evergreen wreaths and swags of past Christmases, à la the Italian della Robbia artwork. Until that time, della Robbia decoration was limited primarily to well-to-do families. So popular was this new Williamsburg decorating style that visitors by the thousands flocked there with cameras in hand, snapping photos to use back home to craft their own della Robbia creations. In the succeeding decades, this della Robbia craze spawned dozens of how-to books, workshops, videos, and television demonstrations. The art form remains popular today.

Several years ago I was smitten with della Robbia myself. Rather than work with wreaths, roping, or swags, I decided to create a table centerpiece instead. (Note: This project is somewhat detailed and advanced.)

🖙 TOOLS: Drill, glue gun, hammer, portable jigsaw, scissors, stapler, wire cutter pliers, pencil

🖙 MATERIALS: Wood (five lengths pine lumber, 1.5" wide and 1.5" thick, one piece 1/2" plywood at least 15" square), window screen, corrugated cardboard (at least 15" square), finishing nails (2.5" long), string, wood screws (1.25" long), floral stem wire (18 gauge), short-needled evergreen sprigs, fresh fruit.

All materials that I use for the basic arrangement, except for the fruit, are recycled. For instance, the wood comes from scraps left over from prior remodeling projects, the screen from an old window in our 112-year-old home, the cardboard from various plant shipments I've received. The Fraser fir greens are from trimmings at the base of this year's Christmas tree. In other years I've used evergreens from our gardens. If you need to purchase items, you can find the first five in any home improvement store. The recycling continues once the centerpiece begins to deteriorate. I either set the complete arrangement outside for the birds to pick on or I cut up the fruit and put it in a feeder.

☞ STEP 1: Prepare materials
Cut four of the five lengths of pine lumber to a length of 18.5". You can do this at home if you have a hand saw or electric table saw, but home improvement stores and lumberyards will generally cut the wood to size for you if you buy it there. Cut the remaining piece to a length of 17.5". Next, cut one end of each of the 18.5" pieces at an angle. To make your guideline for the cut, measure downward 4.5" from the top end along the right-hand edge of the piece and make a pencil mark at the right-hand edge. Take one of the other wood pieces or a ruler and place it at the top of the left-hand edge and align it with the pencil mark you made. Draw the line along the edge of the ruler or wood piece. Cut along the line with a saw or have a salesperson cut it for you at the store. Repeat for each of the three remaining pieces.

Find the approximate center of your piece of plywood and mark it with a pencil. Measure from that point to each of the four sides of the plywood to make sure that you've got at least 15" of wood from the center to the edge. With a hammer, pound a nail into the center spot you marked. Cut a piece of string to a length of about 18" and fold it in half. Tie the two ends together so that the resulting loop is about 7.5" long. Slip the loop over the nail and insert the pencil in the loop. Move the pencil toward the edge of the wood until the string is taut. Keep the string taut and move the pencil forward.

You're now drawing a 15" circle on the wood. Remove the nail. With a portable jigsaw, cut out the circle. Using one of the wood pieces you cut earlier as a guide, draw a line through the center hole of the wood circle so that it bisects the circle. Draw another bisecting line perpendicular to it.

Using your wooden circle as a pattern, place it on the cardboard and trace around it with the pencil. Cut the circle out of the cardboard with a sturdy pair of scissors or kitchen shears.

Cut four pieces of screen to size with the wire cutter pliers. Each piece should be 4.5" wide at the top, 13" wide at the bottom, and 21" from top to bottom (shaped like a triangle with the top cut off).

STEP 2: Assemble materials

Drill a small hole into the center of one end of the 17.5" wood piece. Insert one of the screws into the center of the plywood circle. With the drill, drive the screw into the hole so that the tip just barely comes out on the underside. Place the circle atop the 17.5" piece of wood so that the screw tip fits into the hole you made with the drill. Drive the screw into the piece. Turn the result upright. You should now have a circle with a single piece of wood sticking straight up from its center.

Take each of the four 18.5" pieces, placing them on your work surface so that the angled end faces down, and hammer finishing nails into the top side of each piece. Slant the nails slightly upward as you hammer. The nails should penetrate the wood almost to the underside of the piece. Hammer at least four nails into each piece, placing them where you might want to position a piece of fruit. If there are unused nails once you've positioned the fruit, you can simply cover them with greens or with other decorations such as pinecones.

Next, make sure that the wood piece in the center of the circle is positioned so that each side faces one of the circle's four lines. This will be the center column that supports the four tapered pieces. Attach the tapered ends of the four pieces to the center support with screws, drilling a small hole for each screw first. The non-tapered end of each piece should rest at the outer edge of the circle, centered on the line that runs from the center of the circle to the outer edge. Drill holes and affix the ends with screws. The basic form for the arrangement is now complete.

Taking each one of the screen pieces in turn, attach them to the form with the stapler. Position the narrow top of the screen at the top of the form so that it sticks out over the top about ¾" and the left- and right-hand sides run down the middle of the tapered pieces. There should be enough screen at the bottom so you can tuck it under the circle and staple it underneath. Fold the overlapping top of the screen over and attach it to the top of the form with the stapler. Work your way down the form, first attaching the left-hand side of the screen and then moving over to the next tapered wood piece to attach the right-hand side. Wherever you encounter nails, cut a small slit in the screen with the pliers and slip the screen over the nail. After all the screens are attached, hammer a nail in an upright position into the top of the form, then lay the form on its side, and attach the cardboard circle to the bottom of the wood circle with the stapler. This covers the raw ends of the screen so that they won't catch on a tablecloth or mar the surface of a table.

☛ STEP 3: Decorate form

Attach fruit to the form by impaling it on the nails in any pattern you find pleasing. Once the fruit is in place, you can begin filling in with greens, starting at the top of the form and working toward the base. It's important to use greens with small needles (or leaves) so that they don't overpower the fruit. Attach sprigs of greens with floral wire pins cut to size from the stem wire with the wire cutter pliers. Cut stem wire into 3" or so pieces. Bend each piece in half to form a pin. Position the pin over the bottom end of the evergreen sprig and push the pin down onto the sprig and into the screen to secure it. Overlap sprigs to hide pins and to create a fuller appearance to the arrangement. To fill in with greens over the wood supports, use the glue gun to affix them to the screen.

You can leave your arrangement plain or decorate it with anything that strikes your fancy. I've decorated this particular arrangement with holiday ribbon, attaching it to the base with floral wire pins.

A note about Styrofoam (polystyrene foam): It's tempting to use a large Styrofoam cone for the form, because it's so much easier than building the somewhat complex form I've just described. I've found that most cones are unstable. Having too small a base to support the weight of the fruit, they become top-heavy and have a tendency to topple. Heavy fruit on the end of a nail also needs good support, which Styrofoam doesn't always provide. My concern is that at some point the support may fail, causing the fruit to tumble from the arrangement. It's also very difficult to recycle used Styrofoam cones in the United States. The form I've described and built is very sturdy and stable and can be used over and over for many years to come.

Three Distinctive Wreaths
You Can Make for the Holidays

☞ TOOLS: Glue gun, small hammer, awl. Use the awl to create a pathway for stems when you insert them into a wreath. Insert the awl first and then push the stem gently down into the hole with the awl still in it. You can make the hole larger by manipulating the awl. When the stem is seated, pull out the awl. The straw is flexible and will come back together to close the hole around the stem after you've withdrawn the awl.

Santa Wreath

☞ MATERIALS: 12-inch diameter straw wreath base, dyed club moss (*Lycopodium clavatum*), Styrofoam 1-inch thick, 18-gauge floral stem wire, floral wire pins, wrapping paper, tiny bows, assorted small Santas. You may substitute small-needled evergreens, either fresh or artificial, for the moss.

☞ DIRECTIONS: Begin by arranging the Santas on a flat surface until you find an arrangement that you like. Start with the larger Santas and fill in with smaller ones. Transfer Santas to wreath base, gluing each one in place with your glue gun. Wrap small blocks of Styrofoam with wrapping paper and decorate with bows. Fill in spaces around Santas with packages, leaving some room to add the moss, and attach with glue gun. Attach small overlapping bunches of moss to the wreath with floral wire pins. See instructions for making pins in Step 3 of the directions for the della Robbia centerpiece. Push pins firmly into base to hold moss in place. If pins are difficult to insert, use a small hammer to tap them tightly into the wreath base.

Angel Hair Wreath

☞ MATERIALS: 12-inch diameter straw wreath base, angel hair, white bows, small gold bells, small gold angels, stringed gold pearls, dried lavender sprigs or other fragrant herb (optional).

☞ DIRECTIONS: Attach the dried lavender sprigs or other fragrant herb to the wreath with wire pins (see Step 3 of the directions for the della Robbia centerpiece). Remove angel hair from packaging and tease by pulling it apart both lengthwise and widthwise until it thins to the point where some of it is see-through. Attach one end of strand to side of wreath with wire pins and work your way around wreath, anchoring angel hair to base with pins as you go. Strive for a billowy, ethereal effect, but try to keep the basic round shape of the wreath so that it doesn't look lopsided. Weave pearl string over and under hair and around the back of the base, attaching with pins as you go. Glue bows, bells, and small gold angels to base.

Victorian Wreath

☙ MATERIALS: 12-inch diameter straw wreath base, three dark purple velvet bows with lace edging, three plain white lace bows, small purple strawflowers, green velvet leaves, pinecones (I used white pine), dried double baby's breath (it's showier than single-flowered)

☙ DIRECTIONS: Arrange bows as pictured and attach to wreath with glue or pins. Attach pinecones, stem side down and evenly spaced, with glue. Glue strawflowers to base, primarily around the inside of wreath. Glue leaves to base, with base of leaf tucked in under flower, using two to three leaves per blossom. Fill in with baby's breath. If you prefer, you can substitute any color of your choice for bows and strawflowers.

A Final Touch

Once you've completed a wreath, stand it up on your work surface and decide where the top of the wreath will be to make a hanger on the back. Directly behind the top, insert one of the pins you made, straight into the back and parallel to your work surface. Leave an inch or so of the pin exposed. Bend the pin up toward the top of the wreath so that it forms a right angle to the part that you inserted. Secure the hanger with a dab of glue where the legs of the pin go into the straw. Now you're ready to hang your wreath. (See photo 40 in color section.)

A Gnome Home for Your Garden

Recently, I happened to overhear one of our visitors telling the local media how much she enjoyed the gardens. The young man with the camera and microphone asked her what, in particular, she liked. She replied that she loved all the little plants and things tucked away in nooks and crannies and especially the gnomes. I had to chuckle to myself—we had no gnomes in any of our gardens!

Her comment got me thinking, though: Why don't we have any gnomes? I decided then and there to install a gnome somewhere in our beds. I gave some thought to my gnome project off and on during the winter. By the time spring rolled around, I had a pretty good idea how I wanted to proceed. The gnome had to be partially hidden, so that visitors would discover him unexpectedly. He also had to be integrated into his surroundings so that it looked like he really belonged. I decided on creating the illusion of a gnome home.

The first item I researched wasn't the gnome himself but a door that I could install at the base of a tree to give the appearance that the gnome lived inside. (A tree stump would work well too.) I suspected that I'd find lots more gnomes than I would doors, so I let the door determine the size of my gnome, since I wanted everything to be roughly to scale. The gnome had to be short enough to fit through the door. I also wanted to convey a sense that there were comings and goings into and out of the home. I decided on a cobblestone path that started at the door and connected to a narrow flagstone path in our gardens. For the cobblestones I used flat, smooth pebbles in varying sizes and colors, widely available at craft stores.

The door I ordered turned out to be a big disappointment at first. It was made of one-inch-thick concrete and looked more like a tombstone than a door when I leaned it against the base of the tree I had selected. I toyed with the idea of chiseling a door-shaped hole into the tree and embedding the door in it to bring it more or less flush with the tree bark. Nagging thoughts about doing permanent damage to that beautiful mature spruce finally dissuaded me from trying it. After several more days of thinking about a suitable alternative, I hit upon the perfect solution. I salvaged strips of bark from a neighbor's dead spruce and glued them to the sides and top of the door. Now when I leaned the door against the tree trunk, it actually looked like it belonged.

Once installed, the door, path, and gnome merged beautifully with the garden setting. There was just one challenge left. How would I attract garden visitors' attention to the partially hidden gnome scene? The answer came in the form of a "tree face," those ubiquitous sets of eyes, nose, and mouth that, when attached to a tree trunk, give the tree human attributes. I positioned the face so that it was approximately eye level on the tree trunk and christened the tree Bruce the Spruce. Now, when visitors walk by without noticing the face (or at least not commenting on it), I ask them if they've met Bruce the

Spruce and invite them for a closer look. At that point—so far at least—they discover the gnome home at the base of the tree. Their expressions of delight and wonderment make my day. (See photo 41 in color section.)

A No-Wa-Wa Fountain for Your Garden

What's a no-wa-wa fountain? The term "no-wa-wa" originated several decades ago in a contest by Steve Gander, an Iowa boy who grew up to become one of the top rodeo event promoters in the United States. In 1986, Gander came up with the novel idea of staging the world's biggest beach party in one of his pastures near landlocked Williamsburg, Iowa. He trucked in tons and tons of sand, set up a mechanical surfboard, hired well-known rock bands from the 1950s and '60s, coupled that with a show featuring cars from that era, and began to promote his venture. It was wildly successful, drawing large crowds of sunbathers who loved the combination of sand, old rock songs, and old cars. The contest winner christened the waterless, sandy pasture No-Wa-Wa Beach.

I've borrowed Steve's term, somewhat apologetically, and applied it to my waterless fountain. To use a term currently in fashion, the once-functioning fountain has been repurposed. In its original life, the fountain was solar powered. It had no electrical storage capacity and so it only ran when the sun was shining. The pump, located in the large bowl at the bottom, was somewhat underpowered and somewhat fragile. It lasted all of three months. (I must admit that local raccoons, who often used the large bowl as their wash basin, may have had something to do with the pump's early demise.)

After languishing in our potting shed for a year or so, half-buried under a stack of trays, the fountain caught my eye one day as I was searching for a particular pot. I didn't have the heart to throw out a perfectly good set of terra cotta pieces, but what was I to do with them? I pondered this minor dilemma for several days and came up with a novel solution: instead of flowing water, I would have flowing rocks.

The design is very simple and easy to put together. I bought a bag of pea gravel and spread its contents on our driveway. Next, I got out the garden hose and hosed the rocks down to get rid of the limey dust and other particulate matter clinging to the rocks. When they were shiny clean and dry, I hijacked some of Wilma's wash line cord (the nylon kind) and cut it into appropriate lengths.

I started by sticking one end of the cord into the bottom of the urn at the top of the fountain and placing a heavy rock on top of the cord to hold it in place inside the urn. Then I ran the cord down into the small bowl below it and cut the cord when I reached the bottom center of the bowl. I repeated the procedure with each succeeding bowl, running a length of cord from its center, through the spout, and down into the bottom of the next bowl.

Once I had cut all the lengths of cord, I donned a pair of rubber gloves, got out my caulking gun, and loaded it with a tube of clear silicone caulk. I coated the lengths of rope liberally with the caulk, using my gloved hands to distribute it evenly along the rope sections. As soon as I had coated a section, I draped it across the dry rocks on the driveway. When all the ropes were coated and draped, I removed the gloves and used my bare hands to press rocks on the top sides of the rope sections, making sure that the entire surface of each rope was covered with rocks so the rope was no longer visible. I left the rock-covered ropes on the driveway until the caulk had set and dried.

To assemble the fountain, I gathered the rock-covered pieces of rope and, beginning again with the urn, repeated the earlier rope process, this time weighing the ends of the rope down by piling handfuls of pea gravel on top of them, filling each container almost to the brim. This created the illusion that the rock was actually flowing from one container to the next and — *voilà!* — a new piece of garden art that brought lots of comments from our garden visitors. (See photo 42 in color section.)

GARDENING INDOORS

E VENTUALLY THE GARDENING season must end. I always take my memories of the year's gardens into the winter season with me. But something else carries me through until spring.

Wilma was somewhat skeptical—okay, actually flabbergasted—when I approached her about my yen to build a tropical garden in the middle of three bedrooms on the second floor of our 112-year-old home. (See photo 43 in color section)

We already have three bedrooms, I reasoned, and there are only two of us, so we certainly don't need them all. Besides, there's a fourth room up there that's pretty much vacant. As a temperate zone gardener smitten by tropical plants, I thought this proposal made perfect sense. And so the negotiations began.

"This is absolutely absurd! How are the plants going to survive up there without sunlight? You can't cram them all in front of the windows."

"Fluorescent grow lights."

"How are you going to get those big, heavy pots up there?"

"With a dolly."

"What if the pots leak or overflow and the water comes down through the ceiling into our dining room?" (Much to my chagrin, this actually happened several years later because I forgot to caulk a section of baseboard.)

"I'll think of something."

"Are you planning to have plants all over the room?"

"Yes."

"Well, I need to have a place for my sewing machine and some additional storage space."

"That's fine. I'll figure something out."

As you may have surmised by now, Wilma is truly a saint. Having gained her reluctant consent, I spent the next three weeks or so coming up with design ideas. I'm not very good at drawing up plans on paper, so I worked things out in my head. The time to do this, I soon discovered, was at night in bed before falling asleep. That's when the best ideas came to me.

First, I worked out a space compromise with Wilma. The vacant room measures fifteen feet by fifteen feet. One third would be devoted strictly to plants, one third to a patio and a few more plants, and one third to a sewing area and storage.

The plant and patio parts were easy. I partitioned off the garden third of the room from the patio third by installing a latticework wall with a floor-to-ceiling opening in the middle of the wall to provide access to the garden from the patio. On the patio side of the lattice, I built narrow raised beds filled with rocks and sand that would hold additional potted plants.

In the garden proper, I used the same rock-and-sand mixture. Before putting it down, I exposed the brick on an exterior wall to give some added interest. Then I sealed the wooden floor with roof sealer and covered that with twenty-year rubber pond liner. The sand and rocks would provide a great deal of surface area from which water could evaporate to create a humid atmosphere. Pots could drip and leak to their heart's content, as the water was captured by the out-of-sight rubber barrier.

Next, I dropped the nine-foot ceiling down a foot and a half in the garden, so the potted plants situated on the floor would receive adequate light. I installed a bank of eleven fluorescent light fixtures, using inexpensive shop lights, and spaced them about a foot and a half apart. If you've ever checked out grow-light bulbs that purport to simulate the entire spectrum of sunshine, you know they're very expensive. I solved that problem by purchasing both ordinary grow-light bulbs (wide-spectrum Sylvania GrowLux), which represent primarily the warm spectrum, and cool white bulbs to cover the rest of the spectrum. Each fixture has one of each kind of bulb. An added bonus is the fact that the heat from the warm fixtures is sufficient to heat the entire room, no furnace or heater needed. The lights are on a timer, providing plants with fourteen hours of daylight.

As a final touch, I added a fountain with a small pool. A concealed pump lifts the water from the pool up to a small downward-slanting trough. I filled the trough with activated charcoal, using a few rocks from the floor to retain the charcoal particles. This arrangement serves both to purify and to oxygenate the water as it trickles through the trough and splashes back into the pool below, without the need for an expensive filtering system. I stocked the pool with the obligatory goldfish.

Mindful of the fact that I would be adding a great deal of weight to the floor, I chose brick veneer and ceramic tile for the patio surface and installed them right over the wooden floor. Veneer probably wouldn't have been necessary, given the huge oak and walnut beams used by Wilma's forebears when they constructed this house, but I wasn't taking any chances. I most definitely did not want to hear what Wilma had to say if the entire garden came crashing down into our dining room.

The real challenge was that last third of the room. How on earth would I create a space for sewing and storage, especially one that was compatible with a garden? It was at this juncture that our outside gardens, and in particular the brick cottage located there, were to provide the necessary inspiration. Why not build a cottage?

Given the limited space, I quickly came to the conclusion that I could only build a partial façade. To give the illusion of a complete structure, I built the roof so that it comes right out of the nine-foot ceiling where it meets the wall that separates the garden room from the master bedroom. The roof slopes down gently toward the patio to a six-foot height at the front of the façade. An entryway divides the cottage in half, with the door to our bedroom serving as the (faux) entry door to the cottage.

I wanted to use actual brick for the cottage exterior, given that the real cottage is of brick and that I had exposed the brick on one wall of the garden. Again, visions of a tangle of plants, pots, and plaster on our dining room floor from the added weight dissuaded me from doing so. I settled for brick paneling, accented with rough cedar plank half-timbering.

The portion of the cottage on the left-hand side of the entryway became the sewing room and the portion on the right-hand side the storage room. I added a window and a window box to the sewing room side, so that Wilma could sit and sew while viewing the tranquil garden outside. I finished the interior wall with the same brick paneling that I used for the outside but covered it with stucco, exposing patches of brick here and there as I went. I covered the floor with a remnant of emerald green carpeting.

Inside the storage half of the cottage, I created stucco walls, installed shelves, and painted the bare wooden floor.

Perhaps you're wondering at this point how we get inside the cottage, since the entry door leads into the bedroom. The side walls of the cottage entryway are actually doors into the two cottage halves. From the outside, there's really no way to tell that the doors are there, unless you push against them. I installed spring-loaded hinges, so that the doors would need no telltale handles, would simply push open, and would close on their own.

As I'm writing this, it's dark out, there's a foot or so of snow and ice on the ground, topped off by temperatures in the single digits and winds howling at 40 miles per hour. But in our tropical garden it's still daylight, the temperature is balmy, and the trade winds are calm. You'll have to excuse me now. It's time to have a tall, cool one, catch some rays, and dream of next season's gardens while I peruse a selection from the growing stack of garden catalogs.

BOTANICAL NAMES OF PLANTS
IN THIS BOOK

FRUITS AND VEGETABLES

Apple: *Malus* spp.

Asparagus: *Asparagus officinalis*

Beet: *Beta vulgaris*

Broccoli: *Brassica oleracea* var. *italica*

Cabbage: *Brassica oleracea* var. *capitata*

Cabbage, savoy: *Brassica oleracea* var. *sabauda*

Carrot: *Daucus carota*

Cauliflower: *Brassica oleracea*

Celeriac: *Apium graveolens* var. *rapaceum*

Celery: *Apium graveolens*

Cherry: *Prunus avium*

Chive: *Allium schoenoprasum*

Citron melon: *Citrullus lanatus* var. *citroides*

Corn, sweet: *Zea mays*

Cucumber: *Cucumis sativus*

Currant: *Ribes* spp.

Dandelion: *Taraxacum officinale*

Dill: *Anethum graveolens*

Eggplant: *Solanum melongena*

Endive: *Cichorium endivia*

Garlic: *Allium sativum*

Gooseberry: *Emblica officinalis*

Grape: *Vitis* spp.

Ground cherry: *Physalis minima*

Horseradish: *Armoracia rusticana*

Kale: *Brassica oleracea* var. *acephala*

Kohlrabi: *Brassica oleracea* var. *gongylodes*

Lamb's quarters: *Chenopodium album*

Leek: *Allium porrum*

Lettuce: *Lactuca sativa*

Melon: *Cucumis melo*

Onion: *Allium cepa*

Pea: *Pisum sativum*

Pear: *Pyrus* spp.

Pepper, sweet: *Capsicum annuum*

Plum: *Prunus* spp.

Potato: *Solanum tuberosum*

Pumpkin: *Cucurbita* spp.

Radish: *Raphanus sativus*

Raspberry: *Rubus* spp.

Rhubarb: *Rheum rhabarbarum*

Salsify, European: *Scorzonera hispanica*

Spinach: *Spinacea oleracea*

Squash: *Cucurbita* spp.

Stinging nettle: *Urtica dioica*

Strawberry: *Fragaria* × *ananassa*

String (pole) bean: *Phaseolus vulgaris*

Tomato: *Solanum lycopersicum*

Turnip: *Brassica rapa* var. *rapa*

FLOWERS, SHRUBS, AND TREES

Alyssum: *Lobularia maritima*

Apple, Johnny Appleseed: *Malus domestica* Johnny Appleseed

Apple, Jonadel: *Malus domestica* 'Jonadel'

Apricot: *Prunus armeniaca*

Asparagus fern, vining: *Asparagus verticillatus*

Bluebells: *Mertensia virginica*

Bridal veil: *Spiraea prunifolia*

Bush clover: *Lespedeza thunbergii*

Caladium: *Caladium bicolor*

Canna, Australia: *Canna* × *generalis*
  'Australia'
Canna banana: *Canna* 'Musifolia'
Cattail, dwarf: *Typha minima*
Cherry, wild black: *Prunus serotina*
Chinese seven-son flower tree:
  Heptacodium miconioides
Clematis, sweet autumn: *Clematis*
  terniflora
Clove currant vine: *Ribes odoratum*
Coleus: *Solenostemon scutellarioides*
Columbine: *Aquilegia canadensis*
Coral bells: *Heuchera* spp.
Cornflower: *Centaurea montana*
Corydalis, yellow: *Corydalis lutea*
Cottonwood: *Populus deltoides*
Crown imperial: *Fritillaria imperialis*
Daffodil: *Narcissus* spp.
Daisy: *Leucanthemum vulgare*
Daylily: *Hemerocallis* spp.
Dutchman's-breeches: *Dicentra*
  cucullaria
Elephant ear: *Colocasia* spp.
Fern, Boston: *Nephrolepis exaltata*
Fern 'Fluffy Ruffles': *Nephrolepis*
  exaltata 'Fluffy Ruffles'
Fern, lady: *Athyrium filix-femina*
  'Dre's Dagger'
Fern leaf peony: *Paeonia tenuifolia*
Firetail: *Persicaria amplexicaulis*
Forsythia: *Forsythia* × *intermedia*
Geranium, perennial: *Geranium*
  'Rozanne'
Giant fleeceflower: *Persicaria*
  polymorpha
Glory bower vine: *Clerodendrum*
  thomsoniae
Grape: *Vitis* spp.
Grass, miscanthus: *Miscanthus* spp.

Green velvet alocasia: *Alocasia*
  micholitziana 'Frydek'
Heliopsis: *Heliopsis helianthoides*
'Hilo Beauty' elephant ear: *Alocasia*
  'Hilo Beauty'
Hollyhock: *Alcea rosea*
Hosta: *Hosta* spp.
Hyacinth, Roman: *Hyacinthus*
  orientalis
Hydrangea 'Annabelle': *Hydrangea*
  arborescens 'Annabelle'
Hydrangea 'Limelight': *Hydrangea*
  paniculata 'Limelight'
Iris: *Iris* spp.
Ivy, English: *Hedera helix*
Kiwi vine: *Actinidia kolomikta*
Lady's slipper orchid: *Cypripedium*
  parviflorum var. *pubescens*
Lamb's ears: *Stachys byzantina*
Lamium: *Lamium maculatum*
Larch: *Larix laricina*
Larkspur: *Consolida ambigua*
Lespedeza Gibralter: *Lespedeza*
  thunbergii 'Gibralter'
Lilac: *Syringa vulgaris*
Lotus lily: *Nelumbo lutea*
Maple: *Acer* spp.
Maple, Japanese: *Acer palmatum*
Marigold: *Tagetes* spp.
Mexican Bamboo: *Polyganum*
  cuspidatum
Moneywort: *Lysimachia nummularia*
Morning glory: *Ipomoea* spp.
Nasturtium: *Tropaeolum majus*
Oak: *Quercus* spp.
Osage orange: *Maclura pomifera*
'Painter's Palette': *Persicaria virginiana*
  var. *filiformis*
Pansy: *Viola cornuta*

Pear, Bartlett: *Pyrus communis* 'Bartlett'

Peony: *Paeonia* spp.

Peony, tree: *Paeonia suffruticosa*

Periwinkle, Madagascan: *Catharanthus roseus*

Petunia: *Petunia* spp.

Phlox, garden: *Phlox paniculata*

Pine, white: *Pinus strobus*

Plum, Mirabelle: *Prunus domestica* subsp. *syriaca*

Plum, Stanley: *Prunus domestica* 'Stanley'

Poppy, Flanders: *Papaver rhoeas*

Poppy mallow: *Callirhoe leiocarpa*

Quince, flowering: *Chaenomeles japonica*

Ravenna grass: *Saccharum ravennae*

Rose 'Harrison's Yellow': *Rosa* 'Harrison's Yellow'

Rose 'John Cabot': *Rosa* 'John Cabot'

Rudbeckia 'Henry Eilers': *Rudbeckia subtomentosa* 'Henry Eilers'

Salvia, annual red bedding: *Salvia splendens*

Sansevieria, mother-in-law's tongue: *Sansevieria trifasciata*

Shipova: × *Sorbopyrus auricularis*

Snapdragon: *Antirrhinum majus*

Spruce: *Picea glauca*

Spurge, flowering: *Euphorbia corollata*

Sunflower: *Helianthus annuus*

Sweet pea, perennial: *Lathyrus latifolius*

Sweet potato vine, ornamental: *Ipomoea batatas*

Tulip: *Tulipa* spp.

Tulip 'Rob Vanderlinden': *Tulipa* 'Rob Vanderlinden'

Water lily: *Nymphaea* spp.

Weeping mulberry: *Morus alba* 'Pendula'

Willow, basket: *Salix* spp.

Wisteria: *Wisteria* spp.

Zinnia: *Zinnia* spp.

REFERENCES

Amana Heritage Society. "Amana Heritage Society." http://www.amanaheritage
.org.

Amana Society. *Inspirations-Historie*. Amana, Iowa: Amana Society, 1900.

"Beautiful Legacy: An Iowa Couple Share Vegetable and Flower Varieties from
the Past That Are a Taste of Their Community's Heritage." *Country Gardens* 17,
no. 2 (Spring 2008): 38–43.

Canadian Rose Society. "The Explorer series." The Canadian Rose Society.
http://www.canadianrosesociety.org/CRSMembers/Resources/RosePhotos
/ExplorerRoses/tabid/70/Default.aspx.

Encyclopedia Brittanica Online. "Luca della Robbia." http://www.britannica.com
/EBchecked/topic/156670/Luca-della-Robbia (accessed September 20, 2012).

Family Tree Maker. "John Tweedie." Genealogy.com. http://familytreemaker.
genealogy.com/users/m/c/s/Crystal-Mcspadden-Ontario/WEBSITE-0001
/UHP-0016.html.

Foerstner, Abigail. *Picturing Utopia*. Iowa City, Iowa: University of Iowa Press,
2000.

Herrmann, Fritz H. "Zur Lebensgeschichte des Pflanzenmalers Joseph Prestele."
Wetterauer Geschichtsblätter 28 (1979).

Herrmann, Lore. "Die wichtigsten Giftpflanzen Deutschlands." *Wetterauer
Geschichtsblätter* 26 (1977).

Hoehnle, Peter. "Prestele's Garden." *Pioneer Republican* (November 23, 2008).
Marengo, Iowa.

Hoppe, Emilie. *Seasons of Plenty: Amana Communal Cooking*. Ames, Iowa: Iowa
State University Press, 1994.

Krischik, Vera, Kathryn Bevacqua, and Anne Hanchek. "Selecting Hardy Roses
for Northern Climates." University of Minnesota Extension (2012). http://www
.extension.umn.edu/distribution/horticulture/dg6750.html.

Lankes, Frank J. *The Ebenezer Society*. West Seneca, New York: West Seneca
Historical Society, 1963.

Meehan, Thomas, ed. *The Gardeners' Monthly and Horticulturist, Volume 4*.
Philadelphia: W. G. P. Brinckloe, 1862. Google e-book.

National Garden Bureau, Inc. "National Garden Bureau." http://www.ngb.org
/year_of/index.cfm?YOID=4 (accessed September 20, 2012). Downers Grove,
Illinois.

Rettig, Lawrence L. *Amana Today*. Kansas City, Kansas: Jostens University Press, 1975.

Shambaugh, Bertha M. H. *Amana That Was and Amana That Is*. Iowa City, Iowa: State Historical Society of Iowa, 1932.

Trumpold, Cliff. *Now Pitching: Bill Zuber from Amana*. Middle Amana, Iowa: Lakeside Press, 1992.

University of British Columbia Faculty of Science. "UBC Botanical Garden and Centre for Plant Research." University of British Columbia. http://www.botanicalgarden.ubc.ca/potd/flowering-plants/85.php (accessed September 21, 2012).

Van Ravenswaay, Charles. *Drawn from Nature: The Botanical Art of Joseph Prestele and His Sons*. Washington, D.C.: Smithsonian Institution Press, 1984.

INDEX

alocasias, 58, color photo 8; elephant ear, 58; 'Frydek', 58; 'Hilo Beauty', 58

alyssum, 49, color photo 24

Amana, 9, 10, 11, 13, 14, 15, 16, 17, 22, 25, 27, 29, 30, 31, 33, 34, 35, 36, 37, 38, 39, 40, 41, 42, 43, 44, 46, 47, 53, 55, 56, 57, 59, 60, 66, 79, 80, 82, 83, 88, 89, 92; religion, 1–5

Amana Church Society, 9, 35

Amana Colonies, 9

Amana Heritage Society, 37, 44

Amana Refrigeration, Inc., 9

Amana Society, 3, 4, 7, 9, 10, 22, 42; arts in post-1932 society, 10

apple, 13, 15, 28, 29, 30, 35, 60, 61, 82, 83, 86, 87, 92, 94, 97; Johnny Appleseed, 60; Jonadel, 60

apricot, 59, 94

asparagus, 18, 59, 85

asparagus fern, vining, 16, 70, color photo 26

bamboo, Mexican, color photo 25

bean, 13, 20, 25, 30, 49, 81; lima, 18, 89; navy, 18; string, 18, 47; yellow, 18

baseball, 7, 80

beet, 22, 84

bluebells, 37

bridal veil, 49

broccoli, 49

bush clover, 68; 'Gibraltar', 68, color photo 24

cabbage, 18, 19, 22, 25, 26, 30, 31, 33, 42, 49, 82, 83

cabbage harvest and processing, 40–41; savoy, 22, 63

caladium, 50

canna: 'Australia', 56; banana, 56, color photo 6; Connie Zuber, color photo 37

carrot, 19, 49, 83, 86, 90

cash crops, 22, 42

cattail, dwarf, 58

cauliflower, 19, 49

celeriac, 19, 47

celery, 19, 20, 83, 84, 85, 89, 90, 91

cemeteries, 34–35

cherry, 4, 49; wild black, 49

Chinese seven-son flower tree, 61, 71–72, color photo 19

chive, 19, 82, 85

citron melon, 19, 48

clematis, sweet autumn, 55, 71, color photo 13

clove currant vine, 38–39

cold frames, 18, 19, 21, 22, 23, 25, 26

coleus, 57, 62, 63, 64, 65–66, color photo 7

columbine, 37

Community of True Inspiration (Inspirationists), 1–12, 25, 28, 34, 39, 41, 48, 59

coral bells, 63

corn, sweet, 19–20, 23

cornflower, 49

corydalis, yellow, 60, 78–79, color
    photos 17 and 35
Cottage-in-the-Meadow Gardens, 4,
    49, 52, 54, 65–80; tour, 64–75
cottonwood, 36
crafts, 4, 10; della Robbia centerpiece,
    97–100, color photo 39; gnome
    home, 102–104, color photo 41; ham-
    mered botanical prints, 95–96, color
    photo 38; no-wa-wa fountain, 104–
    105, color photo 42; wreaths, 101–102,
    color photo 40
crown imperial, 63
cucumber, 20, 26, 49, 62
currant, 28, 36, 38, 39, color photo 1

daffodil, 50, 73, color photo 33
dandelion, 20, 26, 44
dill, 20, 25, 30, 84
Dutchman's-breeches, 37

Ebenezer, 2, 3, 8, 11, 12, 13, 15, 25, 35, 37,
    39, 48
Ebenezer Society, 2, 3, 11
eggplant, 50, 81
elders, 2, 3, 4, 7, 8, 11, 13, 15, 17, 35, 36,
    40, 41
endive, 10
evergreens, role of, 34–36

Farm Mennetscher, 9, 17, 23, 31, 33
fern: Boston, 56; 'Fluffy Ruffles', 56–
    57; Lady, 'Dre's Dagger', color photo
    9; vining asparagus, color photo
    26
fern leaf peony, 38, 39
fleeceflower, giant, 72–74; 'Painter's

Palette', 72–74, color photo 28; 'Fire-
    tail', 72–74
food storage, 18, 19, 20, 21, 22, 25, 30, 33,
    46, 48
foraging, 20

Gardebaas, 9, 17, 23, 25, 26, 31, 33, 53
Gardeheisel, 26, 27, 33
Gardelaub, 60, 62, color photo 15
gardening philosophy, 53, 62–64, 78,
    81
Gardeschwestre, 17, 18, 19, 20, 21, 25, 26,
    27, 33
garlic, 22, 84, 85, 92
geranium, perennial 'Rozanne', 75,
    color photo 30
glory bower vine, 58, color photo 8
gooseberry, 36
grape, 14, 20
grass: miscanthus, color photos 19 and
    20; Ravenna, 58, color photo 10
Great Change, 9
Great Depression, 9
ground cherry, 20, 25, 46, 88, 93
Gruber, Eberhard Ludwig, 1

hardscape, 42, 61
Heinemann, Barbara, 36
heliopsis, 68, color photo 23; 'Loraine
    Sunshine', 68, color photo 23
Historical Society of Iowa, 18
hollyhock, 37
horseradish, 20
hosta, 61, 63, 79
hyacinth, Roman, 73
hydrangea: 'Aṇnabelle', 56, 59, color
    photo 12; 'Limelight', 55

insect and disease control, 26, 27, 28, 50

iris, 37; Siberian 'Gull's Wing', color photo 20

ivy, English, 60

kale, 21, 30

Kichebaas, 9, 17, 31

kitchen gardens, 3, 4, 26, 27, 36, 43, 44, 48, 59

kitchens, communal, 3, 4, 5, 7, 11, 17, 18, 19, 20, 21, 22, 24, 25, 26, 28, 30, 31, 33, 45

kiwi vine, 58

kohlrabi, 21

lady's slipper orchid, 37

lamb's ears, 63

lamb's quarters, 26

lamium, 63

larch, 35

larkspur, 49

leek, 22

lespedeza. *See* bush clover

lettuce, 20, 21, 23, 25, 26, 44, 45–46, 62, 83

lilac, 49

Lily Lake, 39–42

lotus lily, 38, 39–42, color photo 2

Ludwig, King of Bavaria, 12

maple, 36, 56; Japanese, 57

marigold, 26, 49

melon, 19, 48, 50

Metz, Christian, 2, 13

moneywort, 63

morning glory, 49

nasturtium, 49

new corporation, 9–10, 42

oak, 36, 61, 109

onion, 17, 21, 22, 25, 26, 30, 31, 32, 33, 35, 42, 44, 47, 48, 49, 82, 83, 84, 85, 89, 90

orchards, 3, 11, 13, 16, 27–28, 29, 36, 42, 59

origins of Amana gardening, 11

osage orange, 36

outsiders, 10, 38, 40

pansy, 49

pea, 21, 49, 69, 85, 90

pear, 13, 15, 28, 30, 56, 59, 61, 95, 97

peony, 37, 38, 39; tree, 76–77, 'Shimani-shiki', color photo 32

pepper, sweet, 22, 50, 81, 82, 83, 84

periwinkle, Madagascar, color photo 24

persicaria. *See* fleeceflower

petunia, 14, 49, 74–75, color photo 29

phlox, garden, 37, 50

pine, white, 34, 35

planting in Old Amana, 4, 18–26, 34; preparation for, 23–26; seed origin, 25

plants, ornamental, 36–42, 53–64, 65–80; favorite, 65–80; Old Amana, 36–42

plum, 15, 28, 59, 60; mirabelle, 59; Stanley, 60

poppy, 66, 82; Flanders, 63, 66

poppy mallow, 69, color photo 25

population, 2, 3, 10

potato, 17, 21, 22, 26, 30, 33, 34, 35, 42, 49, 85, 87, 90; potato harvest, 33

Prestele, Joseph, 11–16, 37, 42; birth, 11;
    death, 16; garden in Amana, 15–16;
    garden in Ebenezer, 13; health, 2,
    13, 15, 16; joins Community of True
    Inspiration, 12; lithography, 12, 13, 15;
    marriage and children, 12. *See also*
    Rawatt; trellis
produce grown in Old Amana, 18–26,
    27–34
pumpkin, 22

quince, flowering, 49

radish, 22, 23, 25, 44, 45, 46, 49, 66, 82,
    83
raspberry, 75
Rawatt, 13, 14, 15, 42
recipes, 82–95; desserts, 93–95; meats,
    91–92; salads, 82–83; soups, 84–85;
    sweet breads and rolls, 86–88; veg-
    etables, 88–90
recreation, 5–7
rhubarb, 28, 29, 94
Rock, Johann Friedrich, 1
Ronneburg, 2
rose, 16, 59, 73; 'Harrison's yellow', 60,
    62, color photo 16; 'John Cabot', 78,
    color photo 34
rudbeckia 'Henry Eilers', 76, color
    photo 31
Russ, Karolina, 12

salsify, European, 22, 25, 44, 47, 88
salvia, annual red bedding, 61, 62, color
    photo 19
sansevieria, mother-in-law's tongue,
    79–80

Schulwald, 34, 35
seed bank, 18, 25, 45–48, 59, 83, 88, 93
shipova, 59–60
snapdragon, 49
South Amana, 3, 7, 35, 39, 42, 43, 53, 55,
    56, 59, 88
spinach, 22, 26, 30, 82, 89
spruce, 16, 34, 35, 71, 103, 104
spurge, flowering, 67, color photos 22
    and 23
squash, 22, 26, 49, 50, 81
stinging nettle, 26
strawberry, 28, 36, 94
sunflower, 49
supertunia, 'Raspberry Blast', color
    photo 29
sweet pea, perennial, 13, 70, color photo
    27
sweet potato vine, ornamental, 63

tomato, 22, 25, 46, 50, 81, 84
tools, gardening, 27,
tourists, 10, 29, 53. *See also* visitors
trellis, 13, 14, 15, 28, 36, 38, 39, 42, 54, 55,
    56, 57, 59, 60, 78, color photo 3
tropical garden, indoor, 107–110, color
    photo 43
tulip, 50, 63, 71; 'Rob Vanderlinden', 77,
    color photo 33
turnip, 22
typical day, 4–5

villages, description and names, 3–4
vineyards, 3, 28, 39
visitors, 7–8, 37, 40, 41, 43, 62, 73, 76,
    102, 103, 105. *See also* tourists

water lily, 58
weeping mulberry, 55, color photo 4
Werkzeug, 1, 5, 36
willow, basket, 28, 36
wine, 3, 28–30, 39, 54
wisteria, 62, 69

work, 3, 4, 5, 8, 9, 13, 15, 17, 26, 27,
    28, 33

yards, 35, 36, 37, 53, 58, 60

zinnia, 49

OTHER BUR OAK BOOKS OF INTEREST

*Always Put in a Recipe and
Other Tips for Living from Iowa's
Best-Known Homemaker*
By Evelyn Birkby

The Biographical Dictionary of Iowa
Edited by David Hudson,
Marvin Bergman, and Loren Horton

*A Bountiful Harvest:
The Midwest Farm Photographs
of Pete Wettach, 1925–1965*
By Leslie Loveless

*Central Standard:
A Time, a Place, a Family*
By Patrick Irelan

Christmas on the Great Plains
Edited by Kenneth Robbins
and Dorothy Robbins

A Cook's Tour of Iowa
By Susan Puckett

*A Country So Full of Game:
The Story of Wildlife in Iowa*
By James J. Dinsmore

Deep Nature: Photographs from Iowa
Photographs by Linda Scarth and
Robert Scarth, essay by John Pearson

*The Elemental Prairie:
Sixty Tallgrass Plants*
By George Olson and John Madson

*The Emerald Horizon:
The History of Nature in Iowa*
By Cornelia F. Mutel

*The Farm at Holstein Dip:
An Iowa Boyhood*
By Carroll Engelhardt

Forest and Shade Trees of Iowa
By Peter J. van der Linden
and Donald R. Farrar

*Frontier Forts of Iowa:
Indians, Traders, and Soldiers,
1682–1862*
Edited by William E. Whittaker

*Gardening in Iowa and
Surrounding Areas*
By Veronica Lorson Fowler

Gardening the Amana Way
by Lawrence L. Rettig

Harker's Barns
Photographs by Michael Harker,
text by Jim Heynen

*Harker's One-Room Schoolhouses:
Visions of an Iowa Icon*
Photographs by Michael Harker,
text by Paul Theobald

*A Home in the West, or, Emigration
and Its Consequences*
By M. Emilia Rockwell

An Illustrated Guide to
Iowa Prairie Plants
By Paul Christiansen and Mark Müller

The Indians of Iowa
By Lance Foster

An Iowa Album:
A Photographic History, 1860–1920
By Mary Bennett

The Iowa Nature Calendar
By Jean C. Prior and James Sandrock,
illustrated by Claudia McGehee

An Iowa Schoolma'am:
Letters of Elizabeth "Bess" Corey,
1904–1908
Edited by Philip L. Gerber
and Charlotte M. Wright

Iowa Stereographs:
Three-Dimensional Visions of the Past
By Mary Bennett and Paul Juhl

Kolonie-Deutsch:
Life and Language in Amana
By Philip Webber

Letters of a German American Farmer:
Jürnjakob Swehn Travels to America
By Johannes Gilhoff

Man Killed by Pheasant
and Other Kinships
By John T. Price

My Vegetable Love:
A Journal of a Growing Season
By Carl H. Klaus

Neighboring on the Air:
The KMA Radio Homemakers
By Evelyn Birkby

Nothing to Do but Stay:
My Pioneer Mother
By Carrie Young

Parsnips in the Snow:
Talks with Midwestern Gardeners
By Jane Anne Staw and Mary Swander

Patchwork:
Iowa Quilts and Quilters
By Jacqueline Schmeal

A Peculiar People:
Iowa's Old Order Amish
By Elmer Schwieder and Dorothy
Schwieder

Pella Dutch:
Portrait of a Language
in an Iowa Community
By Philip Webber

Picturing Utopia:
Bertha Shambaugh and the
Amana Photographers
By Abigail Foerstner

Prairie City, Iowa:
Three Seasons at Home
By Douglas Bauer

Prairie Cooks:
Glorified Rice, Three-Day Buns,
and Other Reminiscences
By Carrie Young and Felicia Young

Sarah's Seasons:
An Amish Diary and Conversation
By Martha Moore Davis

Seasons of Plenty:
Amana Communal Cooking
By Emilie Hoppe

Sunday Afternoon on the Porch:
Reflections on a Small Town in Iowa,
1939–1942
Photographs by Everett W. Kuntz,
text by Jim Heynen

Up A Country Lane Cookbook
By Evelyn Birkby

Visits with the Amish:
Impressions of the Plain Life
By Linda Egenes

Weathering Winter:
A Gardener's Daybook
By Carl H. Klaus

Wildflowers and Other Plants
of Iowa Wetlands
By Sylvan T. Runkel
and Dean M. Roosa

Wildflowers of Iowa Woodlands
By Sylvan T. Runkel
and Alvin F. Bull

Wildflowers of the Tallgrass Prairie:
The Upper Midwest
By Sylvan T. Runkel
and Dean M. Roosa